Inventing, Inventions, and Inventors

Gifted Treasury Series
Jerry D. Flack, Series Editor

Inventing, Inventions, and Inventors: A Teaching Resource Book. By Jerry D. Flack.

INVENTING, INVENTIONS, AND INVENTORS
A Teaching Resource Book

Jerry D. Flack
University of Colorado at Colorado Springs

Illustrated by Adam Burton

1989
TEACHER IDEAS PRESS
A Division of
Libraries Unlimited, Inc.
Englewood, Colorado

TEACHER IDEAS PRESS
A Division of Libraries Unlimited, Inc.
P.O. Box 6633
Englewood, CO 80155-6633
1-800-237-6124

Library of Congress Cataloging-in-Publication Data

Flack, Jerry D.
　　Inventing, inventions, and inventors : a teaching resource book /
Jerry D. Flack ; illustrated by Adam Burton.
　　xi, 148 p. 22x28 cm. -- (Gifted treasury series)
　　Bibliography: p. 133
　　ISBN 0-87287-747-7
　　1. Technology--Study and teaching.　2. Gifted children--Education.
3. Talented students--Education.　4. Inventions.　I. Title.
II. Series.
T65.3.F57　　1989
607'.1--dc19　　　　　　　　　　　　　　　　89-4352
　　　　　　　　　　　　　　　　　　　　　　CIP

*This book is dedicated to my mother, Marian Moyer,
who not only gave me the gift of life, but also
challenged me to use my life in creative, inventive, and
productive ways to make this a better world.*

Table of Contents

Preface

This book is the first volume in the Libraries Unlimited Gifted Treasury Series. What is the Gifted Treasury Series? It is an effort to bring significant and practical teaching and learning strategies and resources to all those concerned with the education of our greatest national treasure: our gifted and talented youth.

Each volume in the Gifted Treasury Series will typically focus upon one subject, but will provide a web of interdisciplinary learning options and approaches which will hopefully promote holistic, significant, and in-depth learning. The subject matter will be carefully chosen to zero in on substantive and meaningful content in order to provide gifted and talented students with challenging learning experiences.

The chief focus of each volume will be devoted to an explication of practical, meaningful, and challenging teaching strategies to assist those concerned with the education of gifted students. Using the specified content, writers will provide educators with tried and proven strategies to develop and enhance gifted students' critical and creative thinking strategies, problem-solving faculties, and reading, writing, research, and independent study skills.

Each volume will additionally accent the critical roles the school library media specialist and the school library media center should play in the education of gifted students. Media is an indispensable tool in the education of gifted and talented students, and the school library media specialist should be seen as a codesigner of curriculum and instruction for gifted students. Each volume in the series will place great emphasis upon recommended resources to be used by both classroom teachers and school library media specialists in the education of these students.

Whenever possible, another hallmark of the Gifted Treasury Series will be the utilization of artwork and product examples by gifted students. Hopefully, the inclusion of such examples will serve as proof that the ideas and strategies suggested in each volume are practical and *do* work.

Future volumes in the Gifted Treasury Series will accent such topics as biography and autobiography, quests and voyages, mysteries and detection, and mythology.

Welcome to the Gifted Treasury Series!

Jerry D. Flack

1

Introduction

Two critical questions need to be addressed by the author and the readers of this book. Both involve the relationship of the book's content and suggested strategies to the gifted and talented school population. The first question is: Why inventions as a content focus? The second question concerns equity: In what ways are the materials and the approaches suggested in the book any different from the materials and approaches which would be deemed as sound instruction for *all* students?

In turn, let us look at each question. Why *inventions* as a course of study? In a stellar article about the teaching of the invention process to gifted and talented students, B. Edward Shlesinger, Jr., states

> It is important to recognize that the entire story of civilization is based on invention. Invention is historically one of the strongest driving forces in human affairs. If children can comprehend invention, they can better understand the past and the present and predict the future more reliably.[1]

Invention is one of the great organizing ideas in world civilization. Therefore, young people, particularly gifted and talented youth with their enormous potential to make significant future contributions to civilization, *should* be engaged in the study of the grand ideas and themes which are the fabric of civilization. Too much of contemporary education for our youth is composed of piecemeal bits of unconnected information. Further, too often the curricula in today's schools separate process and content. Currently there is national concern with *thinking skills* in the nation's schools. While there is surely nothing wrong with teaching thinking skills, there is something very wrong with the assumption that thinking skills can be taught in isolation, divorced from substantive content. A focus on invention allows for a meaningful synthesis of *both* content and process, for significant and in-depth learning, and for the development of worthwhile student products as extensions of classroom learning.

INTERDISCIPLINARY STUDIES

The study of inventions also involves interdisciplinary studies. The science and technology of inventions involves exploration of science with a purpose. Students have the opportunity to see concrete applications of scientific principles when they study and experience the inventing process. In the English classroom, biographies of inventors may be read. One of the key themes in science fiction is the contemplation of the impact of known and hypothesized inventions upon humankind. Inventions are fruitful territory for accomplishing the goals of the social studies. The history of inventions and the impact of inventions are both prime topics of historical study. The impact of past and present inventions, such as those which fueled the industrial revolution, could be the cornerstone of economic studies. Future studies are concerned with such critical issues as the impact inventions being developed today will have on the environment and the way people will live in the future. Geography comes into play when students explore why certain inventions surfaced in particular parts of the world as well as how invention of navigational instruments stimulated exploration. Sociology is the subject focus when students explore how inventions such as the automobile dramatically alter institutions ranging from courtship patterns to where and how people live and raise their families. Ethics issues come to mind when medical inventions are considered.

The list of content connections goes on and on. Indeed, because inventions are such a significant part of our lives, it is difficult to imagine any subject taught in today's schools which does not have direct ties to the broad topics of inventing, inventions, and inventors.

The issue of relevancy can be addressed with the study of inventions. Why do even very bright youngsters sometimes "turn off" school-directed learning? Certainly relevancy is one factor. It is not hard to convince students of the relevancy of inventions to their lives. Every appliance they use, every piece of equipment they encounter, even the clothes they wear had to be invented or designed by someone. The alarm clock which awakens them every morning; the shower equipment, toothbrush, and hairdryer they use; the school bus they ride to school; and the electric lights and heat or cooling equipment in the classroom, all had to be invented by someone who, in turn, based his or her invention on the work of predecessors. Invention is everywhere, *and* it is a relevant and absolutely essential part of our daily lives. As such, it is an important area of study for students.

The second question or concern is: Why is invention a particularly appropriate area of study for gifted and talented students? Probably no human endeavor is more commonly associated with giftedness than the originative act of invention. We marvel at the technological ingenuity displayed by men like Edison and Tesla as well as the artistic daring and innovation of artists like Picasso and Beethoven. The creation of a startling new theory to explain the origin of the universe, the discovery of the curative powers of penicillin, or the invention of an artificial heart are acts of genius universally applauded. It is fitting that gifted children and adolescents who demonstrate such enormous potential for becoming our future discoverers and inventors study inventions, inventors, and the process of inventing. More than 60 years ago, one of the early pioneers in the field of gifted child education, Dr. Leta Hollingworth, wrote of the rationale for including a study of inventions as one of the cornerstones of her curriculum for gifted children:

> We know that civilization depends upon the capable for innovations, for progress. Others can conserve, but only the gifted can originate. Therefore, should not the education of the gifted be education for initiative and originality? But originality depends first of all upon knowledge of what has been done previously, and of how it has been done. To take their place in civilization, therefore, it would seem that the intellectually gifted need especially to know *the history and evolution of the life of civilized man.*[2]

Hollingworth believed it was essential that gifted youngsters have a solid foundation knowledge of the technological marvels of their age and how they came to be before they were sent forth into the world to become inventors and creators themselves. One example of her units of instruction found gifted students studying the raising, preparation, and preservation of foods as practiced by humans throughout history. Primitive means as well as contemporary means were studied.

All this is not to say that the study of inventions is not good for all students. Rather, the omission of the study of inventing and invention from the curriculum particularly impoverishes gifted and talented students. Further, gifted and talented students probably have the maturity and intellectual ability to study inventions and inventing to a much greater degree and depth than students of more normal intellectual abilities. Thus, the strategies and approaches recommended in this book are definitely written with gifted and talented students foremost in mind.

I hasten to add a note of caution. I speak of gifted students without reference to possible quirks and omissions in the ways schools perceive and identify "gifted and talented" students. Indeed, I caution school personnel to always be both circumspect and humble in the identification process. Two profound examples of early genius which went unrecognized by institutions are inventors Thomas Edison and Dr. Robert Jarvik. The abysmal record of the public schools' accommodation of Edison's genius is now so well known it has become part of our folklore. The boy who was too stupid to learn anything or addled became one of the greatest geniuses of all time. In a more modern era, no medical school in the United States would admit Robert Jarvik for matriculation. The future inventor of the artificial heart had to travel to Italy to obtain his medical education.

The study of inventing, inventions, and inventors provides gifted students with countless rich and varied learning opportunities. Careers in engineering and other related fields may be explored. The physics, chemistry, and mathematics of inventions as well as economical, sociological, political, historical, and geographical aspects of invention afford exciting learning opportunities. The study of inventing as a process opens up new worlds of problem solving and skill development for gifted and talented students. Just as students become better writers through provisions for talent development, so too can young people become better and more successful inventors when they have opportunities to *be* inventive. An examination of the lives of inventors sheds light on the need for extreme task commitment if one is to ultimately see one's dreams fulfilled. When students are immersed in the study of inventions and the inventive process, the products they create are not only tangible and worthwhile, they are an automatic and natural extension of content and process.

In forthcoming standards for the education of the gifted and talented in Canada and the United States, The Association for the Gifted, a Division of the Council for Exceptional Children, says this about curriculum for gifted and talented:

> Curriculum for the gifted and talented should include content which is more than information and facts. It should include skills, experiences, and processes. The content needs more academic rigor, real-world orientation and decision-making, and should be interdisciplinary. Content for the gifted and talented should remain abreast of changes in society, such as the area of technology, so that a gap does not occur between reality and curricular content.[3]

It is difficult to imagine a content focus better suited to achieving such standards than that of inventing, inventions, and inventors. The fusion of substantive content, challenging processes, and sophisticated product development may be easily realized in such a study. The currency of studying the latest developments in semiconductors and supercomputers in an effort to bridge the gap between what is learned in the classroom and what is happening in the real world is of undeniable value.

MEETING THE VARIED NEEDS OF GIFTED STUDENTS

A problem confronting teachers of gifted students both in regular classrooms and in special programs is addressing and meeting the varied needs and learning styles of these students. There is generally as much variance *within* the gifted and talented population as there is *between* the gifted students and the general school population. Educators need to recognize that gifted youths often exhibit a remarkable array of preferred learning styles, and that there exist major differences in the *degree* of giftedness. For example, a highly gifted youth with an IQ of 185 is likely to have a quite different set of abilities and needs than another gifted youth whose IQ is about 130. Different kinds of giftedness are also recognized in most definitions utilized by schools. Educators are scarcely meeting the needs of the student gifted in math and science if he or she is pulled from a regular classroom and placed in a program which emphasizes writing haiku poetry. Neither is this same gifted student helped if he or she is placed in the program simply consisting of more ditto sheets with slightly more sophisticated content. It is vital that curricula for gifted and talented students, whether in the regular classroom or in special programs, address both *degree* and *kind* of giftedness. Because invention is such a broad-based topic of inquiry, it is rich with possibilities for explorations which can meet the curriculum needs of all gifted students. Inventions can be approached from a historical perspective by students whose prime area of academic talent lies in that direction. The science and engineering aspects of invention can fruitfully serve students talented in mathematics and the sciences. Because the literature of inventions is so extensive, students representative of all levels or degrees of giftedness can also be accommodated. It is not difficult to find very sophisticated and challenging materials for the highly gifted students in a classroom, nor is it overly hard to simultaneously direct other, more modestly gifted students into challenging but not quite as difficult material.

GETTING STARTED

A CURRICULUM WEB

A very crucial beginning point in a study of inventions with gifted students is to create what reading teachers like to call a curriculum or content web. Figure 1.1 is an example of such a web. The word "invention" occupies the center spot on the chalkboard or overhead transparency. Students initially brainstorm all the things they already know about inventing, inventions, and inventors. This inquiry helps avoid what is surely one of the great crimes perpetrated in education: assumptive teaching. Far too much of the time, teachers "teach" students things they already know or, conversely, leave out crucial skills and vital information based upon the faulty assumption that students have such prerequisites. The webbing activity serves as an excellent diagnostic tool to determine what students already know about a given topic.

An alternative to the webbing tool is featured in figure 1.2 (page 6). Each student silently fills in the blank lines on the acrostic tool, generating ideas about the act of inventing, naming significant inventors and inventions, and listing character traits commonly associated with inventors. After all the students have completed the worksheet, the class discussion proceeds as they note both common and unique responses.

Next, students indicate the things they would like to study further. With these components involved in the webbing process, the teacher has a blueprint around which to build a curriculum which can meet the needs of all the students in the classroom. It should be noted that the teacher need not remain silent in this activity, nor is he or she abdicating responsibility as the professional in

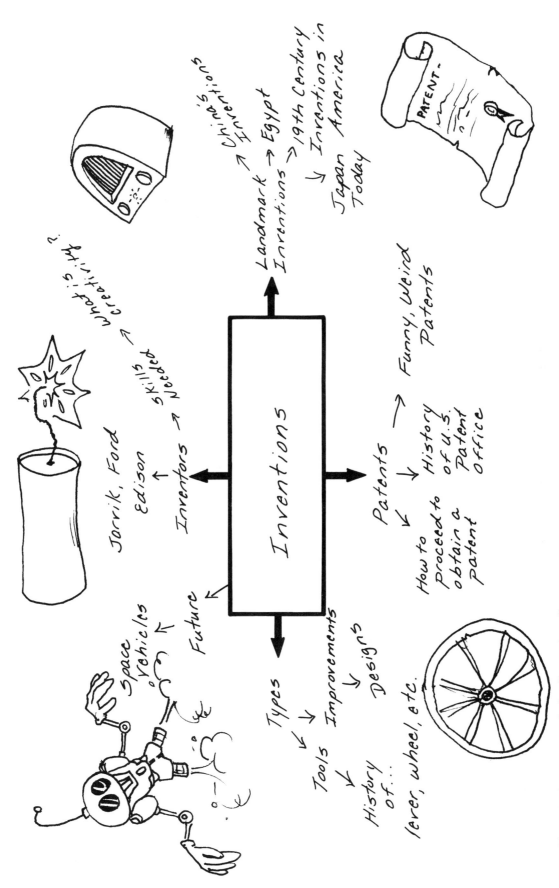

Fig. 1.1. A content web for "inventions."

Write a word beginning with each letter on the left margin which relates in some way to the art of invention, inventors, or famous inventions. After you have written one word for each letter, write additional words for each letter in the word "Invention."

I _____   T _____
  _____   _____
  _____   _____
  _____   _____
  _____   _____

N _____   I _____
  _____   _____
  _____   _____
  _____   _____
  _____   _____

V _____   O _____
  _____   _____
  _____   _____
  _____   _____
  _____   _____

E _____   N _____
  _____   _____
  _____   _____
  _____   _____
  _____   _____

N _____
  _____
  _____
  _____
  _____

Fig. 1.2. An alternative to the content "web."

the classroom. Certainly, the teacher should take part in both guiding students to consider topics they may be omitting as well as decreeing that certain topics are required of all students as part of the classroom accountability.

Concerning accountability, one failing in education which particularly impacts gifted students is the notion that all students must be doing the *same* thing at the *same* time at the *same* pace in order for accountability to be gauged. Teachers argue that they simply do not have time to individualize for 150 students, and/or that they cannot have different assignments for different students because the administration requires a set of specific goals and objectives. The author is sympathetic to both concerns, but asks both teachers and administrators to consider two vital issues. Goals and objectives must be appropriate to the learner if they are to be of any value. In the author's experience, most systemwide goals and objectives are for *minimum competencies* and, as such, are grossly inappropriate for gifted learners. A simple examination of test scores and/or skills levels of gifted students will usually eliminate the requirement for excessive work in areas where it is not needed. A second and vital recognition is that all students, even all gifted students, need not take the same, identical path to meet classroom, school, or district goals and objectives. The example in figure 1.3 serves as an example. The need to satisfy a requirement that students appreciate and demonstrate a knowledge of the history of inventions can be met through a variety of activities. It is important to distinquish activities from objectives. Objectives are measurable translations of goals. There may be many alternative activities, the completion of any one of which will fulfill an objective. In the example provided in figure 1.3, six of an infinite number of possible activities are suggested to meet the single objective. Not all gifted students have to complete the same task in order to meet the teacher's objective.

Goal: Students will appreciate the history of inventions and humankind's continuously evolving search for new ideas.

Objective: Students will complete a culminating project, according to teacher-directed specifications, which demonstrates and exhibits their knowledge of the history and evolution of at least one invention.

Possible Activities to fulfill the objective:

Dramatize a scene of one "Eureka!" experience from invention history.

Create a comic book parody of a famous event in the history of an invention.

Create a slide-tape program about the history of a single invention.

Write and stage a you are there-style interview with the Wright Brothers.

Build a replica of a famous past invention such as the printing press.

Fig. 1.3. A variety of activities can be undertaken to achieve an objective.

A content/process web is a vital component in planning curriculum. Both requirements and options can be specified as an outgrowth of the exercise. Individual, small group, and total class interests and needs will become apparent as the activity progresses, and the possibilities for Individual Educational Plans (IEPs), field trips, speakers, and other important class events will emerge. The use of a web does not mean the teacher waits until students arrive in class to engage in planning. Obviously, the teacher is still the professional in the classroom. He or she decides in advance which concepts, ideas, materials, etc. must be the foundation of the unit on invention. The web adds a new dimension to the planning process in that it tells the teacher what students already know about the topic, what they want to learn more about, and some ways students will enjoy and profit from the learning process. The webbing exercise may also yield important topics and processes the teacher had not considered in the preliminary planning. Students have a role in deciding the "what" and "how" of their curriculum experience. The sharing of one student's interest may also be the necessary spark to guide another student toward significant study and work.

LEARNING CENTERS

Learning centers appear to be a highly advantageous way to meet the individualized needs of gifted students. It does not take a lot of extra time for teachers to create learning centers. Many of the activities suggested in this book are especially well suited to administration via this educational medium. Books and other materials will also be suggested which are appropriate for inclusion in learning centers. However, learning centers should not be the "burden" of the teacher alone. Once the students' interests and talents have been noted in an orientation session, the teacher should allow and encourage students to become a vital part in the creation of classroom learning centers. Remember that gifted students should be creators of materials, not just consumers.

When students enter the classroom for the first time they should see posters on the walls picturing great inventors and inventions. They should be able to immediately thumb through books and pamphlets about inventing. Sample biographies of inventors may be displayed on tables or bookshelves which are reserved for the class invention library. A model of an early airplane may be suspended from the ceiling. There may even be an "inventor's workshop" set up with batteries, wrenches, wire, nails, nuts, bolts, old appliances, clocks, and other tools and artifacts for inventing. An initial invention learning center may contain some simple games and fact sheets with the invention theme and pamphlets from the U.S. Patent Office. Advertisements found in magazines which feature information about inventors (see figure 1.4) may be used to create attractive, informative bulletin boards. The classroom atmosphere will generate excitement and enthusiasm among students, serving as the catalyst for valuable and sustained learning.

THE ROLE OF THE LIBRARY MEDIA SPECIALIST
AND LIBRARY MEDIA CENTER

In an article for *School Library Media Quarterly*, the author argued the case for the indispensable role the school library media specialist must play in the education of gifted and talented students.[4] It is absolutely essential that planning for an inventing/inventions unit be done jointly with the library media specialist. When the library media specialist becomes a full partner in curriculum planning for the education of gifted and talented students and is advised in advance of media needs, he or she can create collections of reference materials for both the classroom learning center and for student use in the Library Media Center (LMC) from existing LMC resources. David V. Loertscher provides excellent models and examples of joint curriculum planning by teachers and

A century ago Edison gave us his name and his patents. It turned into one of his brightest ideas.

Thomas Alva Edison, a true American genius, did more for the world than turn on the lights. As an originator of the light bulb, microphone, phonograph and movie camera, he could be called The Father of Modern Technology. (Photograph: German Museum, Munich)

AEG. More than 100 years of ingenuity behind us.

We at AEG owe Thomas Edison our gratitude as well. The firm he helped found, the German Edison Company for Applied Electricity, became AEG in May of 1887.

While it was a good start, not even Mr. Edison with his perspicacious vision could have foreseen the wonders yet to come. Today AEG ranks among the most advanced technology companies in the modern world.

Here in the U.S., AEG has already become part of your daily life. While our name is not everywhere evident, our stamp is. The average American each day comes into contact, directly or indirectly, with something we're part of. From electronic typewriters and word processors from Olympia down at the office, to satellite TV shows transmitted from space.

AEG

For information write AEG Corp., Dept. 1, Route 22–Orr Drive, P.O. Box 3800, Somerville, NJ 08876.

media specialists in *Taxonomies of the School Library Media Program*. His model, titled "Teachers + Librarians = Co-Designers of Instructions," is especially relevant to colleagues planning an inventions and inventing unit.[5] Some of the best books about the history of inventions are expensive and probably beyond the budgetary limits of classroom teaching materials. The library media specialist may use his or her expertise to help both students and the classroom teacher secure expensive and/or difficult to locate materials which are not part of the current LMC collection.

The writings on invention are abundant and there is considerable range in the quality of these writings. Not only can the library media specialist teach gifted students how to find resources, but also how to critically evaluate resources. The library media specialist's role does not end with the assistance provided to students at the beginning of the research process, via the selection and evaluation of references. Rather, the library media specialist can utilize his or her very considerable research skills to assist students in planning and carrying out research studies. He or she also should serve as a valuable mentor during the product development and reporting stage of the research process. The library media specialist can teach gifted students how to use the Kodak Visualmaker, for example, to create slides for a presentation of research findings. He or she can also assist students in the creation of overhead transparencies, videotapes, and other audiovisual products. Additional suggestions regarding the use of the LMC and the role of the library media specialist will be further addressed in subsequent chapters of this book.

AN INVENTOR'S JOURNAL

The great inventors have kept journals. Leonardo da Vinci's sketchbooks and journals contain drawings for imagined inventions such as the helicopter. In past disputes, an inventor's dated notebook has been the authoritive proof needed to prove ownership of an invention. Throughout the entire unit of study with inventions, all students should be encouraged, if not required, to maintain a notebook or journal. Writing in the journal may commence on the first day of class with prompts such as:

What do you think an invention is?

Who is/was the greatest inventor of all time?

What is the greatest invention ever created?

Make a list of all the things in this classroom which had to be invented.

The journal/notebook should contain notes and reactions to biographies of inventors which students read, films they view in or out of class, and speakers they hear. It should be the repository for their brainstorming to come up with ideas about projects or inventions. To keep in the real spirit of being an inventor, caution students to date all entries in order to document the origins of their ideas. The journal is definitely the place to sketch diagrams of their ideas for inventions and to work out related mathematical problems. Neatness is not the priority. *Creativity is messy!* From the first day, the inventor's notebook should be an integral part of every student's participation in class. Incidentally, one way the author has found journals to be useful in classroom communication is the "two-way" journal procedure in which the students' journals function as a written dialogue mechanism. Students turn in their journals periodically and the teacher not only reads, but responds by writing both in the margins and through new entries. In this way, the teacher makes suggestions; recommends new books, sources, or courses of action to try; asks questions; and shares his or her own interests and experiences relative to the topic. Students enjoy the personal attention and often realize for the first time that the teacher *is* paying attention to their work and behavior, and is genuinely interested in their ideas and progress in the class. This personalization is just as vital for egos of gifted students as for any other students.

RESOURCES

This book is very much about resources. Throughout the text, books, films, organizations and other learning resources will be recommended. At this juncture, several exceptional resources are cited that should be sampled by teachers before starting the unit. These appear to the author to be essential materials to have in the classroom *before* the study of inventing, inventions, and inventors is commenced. They are listed here so that teachers may order and purchase these materials well in advance of their first class. As the interests and needs of students emerge during the unit, many other resources can be added. A more complete resource bibliography appears at the end of the book.

The activities and approaches in the remainder of this book may be approached and utilized in any order. There is no right or correct way to structure the use of the text. The author uses a convenient, chronological order, but other educators may choose to use the materials in a quite different, but well-reasoned order. Above all, enjoy. Many studies suggest that the thing gifted students most prize in their teachers is enthusiasm.[6] Invention is an exciting and exhilarating topic. Hopefully, this book will cause enthusiastic teachers of gifted students to teach with even greater joy and verve.

Books

Caney, Steven. *Steven Caney's Invention Book.* New York: Workman Publishing Company, Inc., 1985.

Caney tells students how to set up their own inventor's workshop. He additionally provides fascinating and entertaining accounts about the origins of many commonplace inventions.

Giscard d'Estaing, Valerie-Ann. *The World Almanac Book of Inventions.* New York: World Almanac Publications, 1985.

This oversized, but inexpensive book is an encyclopedia of the history and development of inventions.

Macaulay, David. *The Way Things Work.* Boston: Houghton Mifflin Company, 1988.

The author and illustrator of the three books *Castle*, *Cathedral*, and *Pyramid*, turns his attention to the working of machines in this excellent resource book. Macaulay utilizes a woolly mammoth to both entertain and instruct readers about how today's technology works and how it came to be.

Shlesinger, B. Edward, Jr. *How to Invent: A Text for Teachers and Students.* Alexandria, Va.: IFI/Plenum Data Corporation, 1985.

Shlesinger provides the fundamentals, definition, rationale, procedures, and processes of invention, and suggestions for teaching inventing.

Vare, Ethlie Ann, and Greg Ptachek. *Mothers of Invention: From the Bra to the Bomb: Forgotten Women & Their Unforgettable Ideas*. New York: William Morrow & Company, Inc., 1988.

Fifty percent of the population cannot and must not be ignored. *Mothers of Invention* is not the best book ever written about invention, but it is a giant step in the right direction toward correcting the erroneous notion that men are the only inventors.

Periodicals

American Heritage of Invention and Technology. Three issues published each year. For subscription information write: American Heritage of Invention and Technology, Subscription Office, P.O. Box 6485, Syracuse, NY 13217.

This periodical is devoted to recounting the history of inventions, breakthroughs, and discoveries which have altered the way people live. Advancements in fields as diverse as medicine and astronomy are portrayed.

Inventor's Digest. Published six times each year. Write: Affiliated Inventors Foundation, 2132 Bijou Street, Colorado Springs, CO 80909-5950.

This is a trade publication. Articles about inventors, inventions, patents, and announcements of invention fairs are featured.

Selected Articles

Hughes, Thomas P. "How Did the Heroic Inventors Do It?" *American Heritage of Invention and Technology* 1, no. 2 (Fall 1985): 18-25.

The inventing strategies and techniques of famous inventors such as Edison, Tesla, and Sperry are explored in this very readable article.

Moser, Penny Ward. "Dreams, Schemes, and 3,300 Mousetraps." *Discover* 6, no. 12 (December 1985): 72-79.

The everyday workings of the U.S. Patent Office are explored in this first-rate, highly informative article.

Shlesinger, B. Edward, Jr. "An Untapped Resource of Inventors: Gifted and Talented Children." *Elementary School Journal* 82, no. 3 (January 1982): 215-20.

Shlesinger has written widely and often about the subject of inventing with gifted children. This article is an excellent representation of his writings.

U.S. Government Documents

U.S. Department of Commerce, Patent and Trademark Office. *General Information Concerning Patents: A Brief Introduction to Patent Matters*, 1986.

The information most students need to know about patents is contained in this inexpensive pamphlet.

U.S. Department of Commerce, Patent and Trademark Office. *The Story of the U.S. Patent and Trademark Office*, 1981.

This pamphlet provides an interesting and informative chronology of major events in the development of inventions and patents for nearly 200 years of American history.

Both documents may be ordered from:

U.S. Government Printing Office
Superintendent of Documents
Washington, DC 20402

Videos

Gizmo. New Line Cinema, 1977. (Distributed by Warner Home Video.) Check local video stores and the film collection of local libraries for availability.

Here is a wonderful documentary film about the crazy world of inventions. It is simultaneously a unique social history of the twentieth century.

How to Invent. IFI/Plenum Data Corporation (302 Swann Avenue, Alexandria, VA 22301), 1985.

Shlesinger's *How to Invent* is offered as a video as well as in print format.

To Fly! Conoco, Inc. (1007 Market Street, Wilmington, DE 19898), 1976.

This twenty-seven-minute film was the premier film seen at the Smithsonian Institution's National Air and Space Museum. It portrays the evolution of America's air and space developments.

The film collections of school systems, universities, and some larger public libraries are likely to contain film biographies of the more famous inventors such as Thomas Edison, Alexander Graham Bell, and Henry Ford. These film libraries may also have films on inventions, inventing, or related fields such as creative problem solving. Again, wise teachers of gifted students will consult the school library media specialist in tracking down such resources.

NOTES

[1]B. Edward Shlesinger, Jr., "An Untapped Resource for Inventors: Gifted and Talented Children," *The Elementary School Journal* 82, no. 3 (January 1982): 219.

[2]Leta S. Hollingworth, *Gifted Children: Their Nature and Nurture* (New York: The Macmillan Company, 1926), 313.

[3]Beverly N. Parkes, "First Steps toward Program Standards in Educating the Gifted and Talented" (An unpublished document prepared as an outcome of The Association for Gifted Symposium I, Fort Worth, Texas, March 13-14, 1987), 15-18.

[4]Jerry D. Flack, "A New Look at a Valued Partnership: The Library Media Specialist and Gifted Students," *School Library Media Quarterly* 14, no. 3 (Summer 1986): 174-79.

[5]David V. Loertscher, *Taxonomies of the School Library Media Program* (Englewood, Colo.: Libraries Unlimited, 1988), 59-86.

[6]Barbara Clark, *Growing Up Gifted*, 3rd ed. (Columbus, Ohio: Merrill Publishing Company, 1988), 534-45. Dr. Clark provides an excellent overview of the research on teacher effectiveness with gifted students.

2

The Past

WHY HISTORY?

In *The 100: A Ranking of the Most Influential Persons in History*, author Michael H. Hart ranks Sir Isaac Newton as the second most influential person, between Mohammed and Jesus Christ, ever to live on this planet. The rationale Hart gives for Newton's extraordinarily high ranking is that Newton is the father of modern science and modern science and technology has forever changed humanity.[1] Even though Newton is so recognized, the great scientist wrote these famous lines in a letter to Robert Hooke in 1675:

> If I have seen further (than you and Descartes) it is by standing upon the shoulders of Giants.[2]

Newton paid homage to the work of those who had gone before him. His point is worth noting. How can any of today's youth, even the most gifted, hope to contribute to the present and the future without knowledge of the inventive inheritance which is theirs?

Some gifted students thrive on historical subject matter and will readily immerse themselves in the history and background of inventions. They will eagerly read biographies of inventors and delight in learning about the evolution of specific inventions. They will be the class invention historians. Others, more mechanically inclined, may want to dodge the history lesson and get on with the reality of actually inventing. They want to build the better mousetrap *now*.

The thrust of this text is that all kinds of gifts and all types of learning styles can be accommodated when broad-based, inclusive topics and themes such as invention are utilized. It is the author's contention that all students should have at least a cursory knowledge of the past in order to appreciate the fact that they do not live in caves and are not starting from a zero point in their rush to invent. In this, as in all chapters, it is not expected that each student will engage in or complete all activities suggested. Rather, what is provided herein is a wide variety of ways and means to learn the history and background of inventors and inventions.

HISTORY OF THE U.S. PATENT OFFICE

The issue of patents for new discoveries
has given a spring to invention beyond
my conception.

> — Thomas Jefferson

The Patent System added the fuel of interest to
the fire of genius.

> — Abraham Lincoln,
>   Recipient of Patent No. 6469

A country without a patent office and good
patent laws is just a crab and can't
travel anyway but sideways and backways.
> — "Sir Boss" *A Connecticut Yankee In*
>   *King Arthur's Court*
>
> — Samuel L. Clemens,
>   Recipient of three U.S. Patents

In Philadelphia in 1787, the founding fathers of the United States of America provided for the U.S. Patent Office in the Constitution. Article I, Section 8 states:

> Congress shall have power To promote the Progress of Science and useful Arts, by securing for limited Times to Authors and Inventors the exclusive Right to their respective Writings and Discoveries.

In April 1790, President George Washington signed into the law the bill which laid the groundwork for the U.S. Patent Office. For nearly two centuries the Patent Office has screened millions of inventions and has provided patents to protect the works of such geniuses as Alexander Graham Bell, Thomas Alva Edison, and the Wright Brothers.

All students should have some knowledge and familiarity with the history of the Patent Office. Some students with strong interests in history and the law will want to make much more extensive studies of this unique institution. This chapter covers the history of the Patent Office. For instructional plans regarding the securing of a patent, see chapter 4, "The Present."

One way to begin a study of the U.S. Patent Office is with a Patent Office trivia game (figure 2.1), which may be used orally with the entire class as an introduction to a lesson about the Patent Office, or reproduced and placed in the invention learning center. The questions (and answers) in figure 2.1 are based upon information found in *The Story of the U.S. Patent and Trademark Office* (1981), a U.S. government document.[3]

In April 1988, the U.S. Patent Office extended for the first time a patent for an animal. Harvard University received Patent No. 4,736,856 for a genetically engineered mouse born with genes to promote cancer cell growth.[4] Until this history-making event, patents had been awarded in three basic areas: utility patents, design patents, and plant patents. Most famous inventions, including Bell's telephone and Edison's phonograph, fall into the first category. An example of a design patent is Patent No. 11,023 issued February 18, 1879 to A. Bartholdi (see figure 2.3) for a statue design which has come to be known as the Statue of Liberty. In December 1976, James Mikkelsen of Ashtabula, Ohio, received Plant Patent No. 4,000 for a "new and distinctive cultivar of poinsettia plant, botanically known as *Euphorbia pulcherrima*."[5]

U.S. Patent Office History Trivia Game

Who signed the first patent bill in human history into law? (George Washington)

Name the man who received a patent for a cotton gin in 1794. (Eli Whitney. Note: Some historians argue that, in truth, the cotton gin was the inspiration of Whitney's landlady Catherine Greene. Whitney built the prototype and secured the patent.)

What was unique about the 1809 patent granted to Mary Kies of Killingly, Connecticut? (First patent ever granted to a woman. Note: Ethlie Vare and Greg Ptacek, authors of *Mothers of Invention*, claim this accomplishment is erroneously attributed to Mary Kies. They state that the first patent was issued to Mrs. Samuel Slater in 1793 for cotton sewing thread.)

Name the U.S. president who received a patent in 1849 for a navigational instrument. (Abraham Lincoln)

Who received a patent in 1834 for a mechanical reaper? (Cyrus H. McCormick)

What famous American author received a patent in 1871 for pants suspenders? (Mark Twain or Samuel L. Clemens. He received two more patents; one in 1873 and another in 1885.)

For what landmark invention did Thomas A. Edison of Menlo Park, New Jersey, secure a patent on January 27, 1880? (An electric lamp)

Guglielmo Marconi received a patent for wireless telegraphy in 1898. Name the country of which he was a subject. (Italy)

In 1973, the National Inventor's Hall of Fame was founded. Name the person who became the first inductee. (Thomas A. Edison)

Fig. 2.1. Facts for game from *The Story of the U.S. Patent and Trademark Office* (Washington, D.C.: U.S. Department of Commerce, 1981).

Figures 2.2 through 2.4 are actual reproductions of patents granted by the U.S. Patent Office. They may be reproduced for classroom use. These reprints help illustrate what a patent is as well as provide a pictorial slice of history.

Many individual and small group activities can stem from an introductory lesson about patent history. Students should note significant dates for inclusion on a classroom time line of invention history. Some students may want to begin a separate time line exclusively devoted to historical events associated with the U.S. Patent Office.

A design invention would be an original calendar based upon the history of the Patent Office. The twelve main illustrations might be of famed inventions or inventors which have received U.S. Patents. Significant dates can be highlighted throughout the year. For example, students might note events and dates such as these:

January 28 (1873)	Louis Pasteur receives U.S. Patent No. 132,245 for "improvements in the process of making beer."
March 7 (1876)	Alexander Graham Bell receives patent No. 174,465 for the telephone.
March 20 (1960)	First patent granted for lasers.
July 13 (1898)	Guglielmo Marconi of Italy receives U.S. Patent No. 586,193 for wireless telegraphy.
November 11 (1931)	Albert Einstein of Berlin receives U.S. Patent No. 1,781, 541 for "an apparatus for producing refrigeration."
December 19 (1871)	Mark Twain (Samuel L. Clemens) receives Patent No. 121,992 for "an improvement in adjustable and detachable straps for garments."

Please note that the production and sale of such a calendar would make an excellent project for the class to make the money for some of the costs of the patent processing for a student's invention or to provide funds for a field trip to a science and technology museum.

Two high recommended books about the U.S. Department of Commerce Patent and Trademark Office which were cited in chapter 1 are:

U.S. Department of Commerce, Patent and Trademark Office, *The Story of the United States Patent and Trademark Office*. Washington, D.C.: U.S. Government Printing Office, 1981.

U.S. Department of Commerce, Patent and Trademark Office, *General Information Concerning Patents: A Brief Introduction to Patent Matters*. Washington, D.C.: U.S. Government Printing Office, 1986.

(Text continues on page 27.)

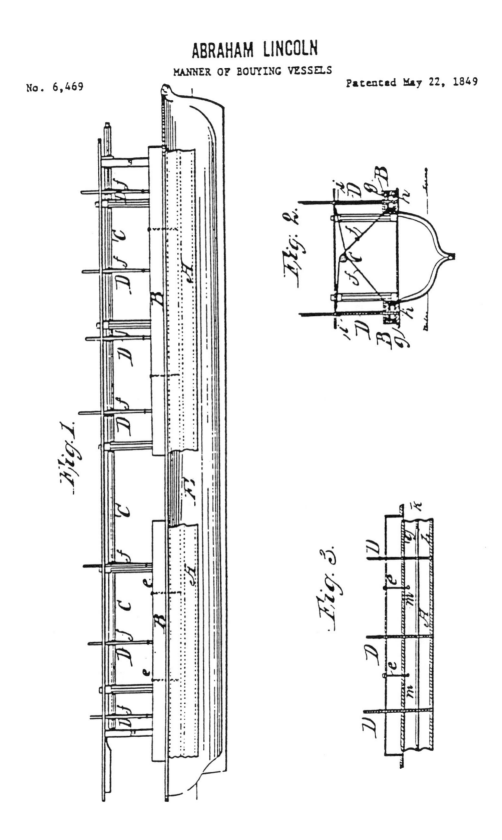

ABRAHAM LINCOLN

MANNER OF BOUYING VESSELS

No. 6,469

Patented May 22, 1849

Fig. 2.2. A utility patent granted to Abraham Lincoln.

(Fig. 2.2 continues on page 20.)

Fig. 2.2—*Continued*

UNITED STATES PATENT OFFICE

ABRAHAM LINCOLN, OF SPRINGFIELD, ILLINOIS.

BUOYING VESSELS OVER SHOALS.

Specification forming part of Letters Patent No. 6,469, dated May 22, 1849; application filed March 10, 1849.

To all whom it may concern:

Be it known that I, Abraham Lincoln, of Springfield, in the County of Sangamon, in the State of Illinois, have invented a new and improved manner of combining adjustable buoyant air chambers with a steamboat or other vessel for the purpose of enabling their draught of water to be readily lessened to enable them to pass over bars, or through shallow water, without discharging their cargoes; and I do hereby declare the following to be a full, clear, and exact description thereof, reference being had to the accompanying drawings making a part of this specification. Similar letters indicate like parts in all the figures.

The buoyant chambers A, A, which I employ, are constructed in such a manner that they can be expanded so as to hold a large volume of air when required for use, and can be contracted into a very small space and safely secured as soon as their services can be dispensed with.

Fig. 1, is a side elevation of a vessel with the buoyant chambers combined therewith, expanded;

Fig. 2, is a transverse section of the same with the buoyant chambers contracted.

Fig. 3, is a longitudinal vertical section through the centre of one of the buoyant chambers, and the box B, for receiving it when contracted, which is secured to the lower guard of the vessel.

The top *g*, and bottom *h*, of each buoyant chamber, is composed of plank or metal, of suitable strength and stiffness, and the flexible sides and ends of the chambers, are composed of india-rubber cloth, or other suitable water-proof fabric, securely united to the edges and ends of the top and bottom of the chambers.

The sides of the chambers may be stayed and supported centrally by a frame *k*, as shown in Fig. 3, or as many stays may be combined with them as may be necessary to give them the requisite fullness and strength when expanded.

The buoyant chambers are suspended and operated as follows: A suitable number of vertical shafts or spars D, D, are combined with each of the chambers, as represented in Figs. 2 and 3, to wit: The shafts work freely in apertures formed in the upper sides of the chambers, and their lower ends are permanently secured to the under sides of the chambers: The vertical shafts or spars (D,D,) pass up through the top of the boxes B, B, on the lower guards of the vessel, and then through its upper guards, or some other suitable support, to keep them in a vertical position.

The vertical shafts (D, D,) are connected to the main shaft C, which passes longitudinally through the centre of the vessel—just below its upper deck—by endless ropes *f, f*, as represented in Fig. 2: The said ropes, *f, f*, being wound several times around the main shaft C, then passing outwards over sheaves or rollers attached to the upper deck or guards of the vessel, from which they descend along the inner sides of the vertical shafts or spars D, D, to sheaves or rollers connected to the boxes B, B, and thence rise to the main shaft (C,) again.

The ropes *f, f*, are connected to the vertical shafts at *i. i*, as shown in Figs. 1 and 2. It will therefore be perceived, that by turning the main shaft C, in one direction, the buoyant chambers will be expanded into the position shown in Fig. 1; and by turning the shaft in an opposite direction, the chambers will be contracted into the position shown in Fig. 2.

In Fig. 3, *e. e*, are check ropes, made fast to the tops of the boxes B, B, and to the upper sides of the buoyant chambers; which ropes catch and retain the upper sides of the chambers when their lower sides are forced down, and cause the chambers to be expanded to their full capacity. By varying the length of the check ropes, the depth of immersion of the buoyant chambers can be governed. A suitable number of openings *m, m*, are formed in the upper sides of the buoyant chambers, for the admission and emission of air when the chambers are expanded and contracted.

The ropes *f, f*, that connect the main shaft C, with the shafts or spars D, D, (rising from

2   6.469

the buoyant chambers,) may be passed from one to the other in any direction that may be deemed best, and that will least incommode the deck of the vessel; or other mechanical means may be employed as the medium of communication between the main shaft and the buoyant chambers, if it should be found expedient.

I shall generally make the main shaft C. in as many parts as there are corresponding pairs of buoyant chambers. so that by coupling the sections of the shaft together, the whole of the chambers can be expanded at the same time, and by disconnecting them, either pair of chambers can be expanded, separately from the others as circumstances may require.

The buoyant chambers may be operated by the power of the steam engine applied to the main shaft C. in any convenient manner, or by man power.

Where the guards of a vessel are very high above the water, the boxes B. B. for the reception of the buoyant chambers when contracted. may be dispensed with, and the chambers be contracted by drawing them against the under side of the guards. Or. protecting cases may be secured to the under sides of the guards for the reception of the buoyant chambers when contracted.

When it is desired to combine my expansible buoyant chambers with vessels which have no projecting guards; shelves or cases must be strongly secured to their sides for the reception of the buoyant chambers.

I wish it to be distinctly understood, that I do not intend to limit myself to any particular mechanical arrangement, in combining expansible buoyant chambers with a vessel, but shall vary the same as I may deem expedient, whilst I attain the same end by substantially the same means.

What I claim as my invention and desire to secure by letters patent, is the combination of expansible buoyant chambers placed at the sides of a vessel, with the main shaft or shafts C, by means of the sliding spars or shafts D, which pass down through the buoyant chambers and are made fast to their bottoms, and the series of ropes and pullies, or their equivalents, in such a manner that by turning the main shaft or shafts in one direction, the buoyant chambers will be forced downwards into the water and at the same time expanded and filled with air for buoying up the vessel by the displacement of water; and by turning the shaft in an opposite direction, the buoyant chambers will be contracted into a small space and secured against injury.

A. LINCOLN.

Witness:
Z. C. ROBBINS,
H. H. SYLVESTER.

UNITED STATES PATENT OFFICE.

AUGUSTE BARTHOLDI, OF PARIS, FRANCE.

DESIGN FOR A STATUE.

Specification forming part of Design No. 11,023, dated February 18, 1879; application filed January 2, 1879.
[Term of patent 14 years.]

To all whom it may concern:

Be it known that I, AUGUSTE BARTHOLDI, of Paris, in the Republic of France, have originated and produced a Design of a Monumental Statue, representing "Liberty enlightening the world," being intended as a commemorative monument of the independence of the United States; and I hereby declare the following to be a full, clear, and exact description of the same, reference being had to the accompanying illustration, which I submit as part of this specification.

The statue is that of a female figure standing erect upon a pedestal or block, the body being thrown slightly over to the left, so as to gravitate upon the left leg, the whole figure being thus in equilibrium, and symmetrically arranged with respect to a perpendicular line or axis passing through the head and left foot. The right leg, with its lower limb thrown back, is bent, resting upon the bent toe, thus giving grace to the general attitude of the figure. The body is clothed in the classical drapery, being a stola, or mantle gathered in upon the left shoulder and thrown over the skirt or tunic or under-garment, which drops in voluminous folds upon the feet. The right arm is thrown up and stretched out, with a flamboyant torch grasped in the hand. The flame of the torch is thus held high up above the figure. The arm is nude; the drapery of the sleeve is dropping down upon the shoulder in voluminous folds. In the left arm, which is falling against the body, is held a tablet, upon which is inscribed "4th July, 1776." This tab-let is made to rest against the side of the body, above the hip, and so as to occupy an inclined position with relation thereto, exhibiting the inscription. The left hand clasps the tablet so as to bring the four fingers onto the face thereof. The head, with its classical, yet severe and calm, features, is surmounted by a crown or diadem, from which radiate divergingly seven rays, tapering from the crown, and representing a halo. The feet are bare and sandal-strapped.

This design may be carried out in any manner known to the glyptic art in the form of a statue or statuette, or in alto-relievo or bass-relief, in metal, stone, terra-cotta, plaster-of-paris, or other plastic composition. It may also be carried out pictorially in print from engravings on metal, wood, or stone, or by photographing or otherwise.

What I claim as my invention is—

The herein-described design of a statue representing Liberty enlightening the world, the same consisting, essentially, of the draped female figure, with one arm upraised, bearing a torch, while the other holds an inscribed tablet, and having upon the head a diadem, substantially as set forth.

In testimony whereof I have signed this specification in the presence of two subscribing witnesses.

A. BARTHOLDI

Witnesses:
O. TÉRINIER,
COTTIN.

Fig. 2.3. A design patent granted to Auguste Bartholdi. (See illustration p. 23.)

DESIGN.

A. BARTHOLDI.
Statue.

No. 11,023.   Patented Feb. 18, 1879.

LIBERTY ENLIGHTENING THE WORLD.

Eli Whitney   COTTON GIN   Patented March 14, 1794

THE UNITED STATES OF AMERICA

To all to whom these Letters Patent shall come:

Whereas Eli Whitney a Citizen of the State of Massachusetts, in the United States, hath alledged that he has invented a new and useful improvement in the mode of Ginning Cotton, which improvement has not been known or used before his application, has made oath, that he does verily believe, that he is the true inventor or discoverer of the said Improvement, has paid into the Treasury of the United States, the sum of thirty dollars, delivered a receipt for the same, and presented a petition to the Secretary of State, signifying a desire of obtaining an exclusive property in the said Improvement, and praying that a Patent may be granted for that purpose: These are therefore, to grant according to law to the said Eli Whitney, his heirs, administrators or assigns, for the term of fourteen years from the sixth day of November last, the full and exclusive right and liberty of making, constructing, using and vending to others to be used the said improvement, a Description whereof is given in the words of the said Eli Whitney himself in the Schedule hereto annexed, and is made a part of these presents.

In testimony whereof, I have caused these Letters to be made Patent, and the Seal of the United States to be hereunto affixed.

(Seal of the United States)

Given under my hand, at the City of Philadelphia, this fourteenth day of March, in the year of our Lord, one thousand seven hundred and ninety four, and of the Independence of the United States of America, the Eighteenth.

Geo: Washington.

By the President

Edm: Randolph

City of Philadelphia to wit:

I do hereby certify, that the foregoing Letters Patent were delivered to me on the fourteenth day of March in the year of our Lord one thousand seven hundred and ninety four to be examined; that I have examined the same and find them conformable to law. And I do hereby return the same to the Secretary of State, within fifteen days from the date aforesaid; to wit, on this same fourteenth day of March in the year aforesaid.

Wm. Bradford, *Atty Gen. U.S.*

Fig. 2.4. A utility patent granted to Eli Whitney.

Eli Whitney   COTTON GIN   Patented March 14, 1794

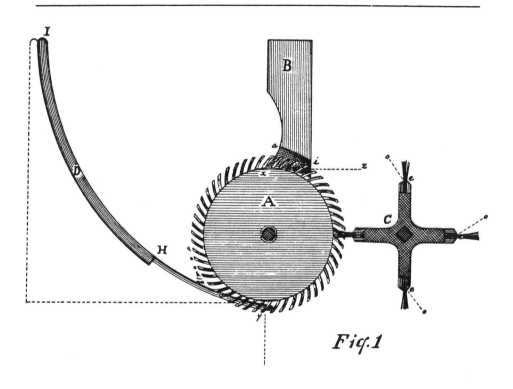

Fig.1

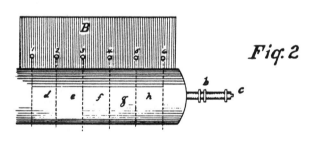

Fig. 2

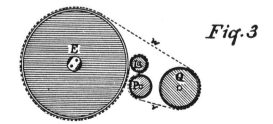

Fig. 3

(Fig. 2.4 continues on page 26.)

Fig. 2.4—*Continued*

Eli Whitney   COTTON GIN   Patented March 14, 1794

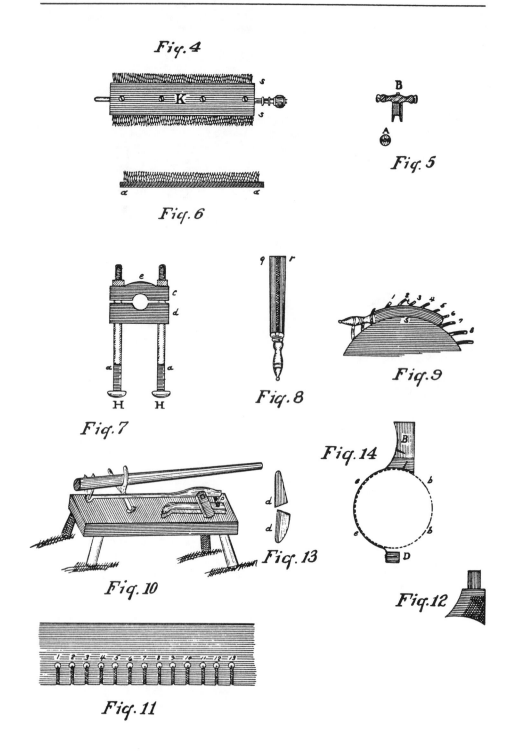

THE IMPACT OF INVENTORS

As mentioned earlier, Hart's *The 100: A Ranking of the Most Influential Persons in History* is an intriguing book in which the author examines the contributions of men and women throughout all known history. It provides short biographical sketches of the 100 people he deems to have been the most influential. Hart offers a rationale for the placements or rankings given to each person. Though brief, the biographical segments are generally quite informative and prove especially useful to teachers because they are short enough to be read to classes. Two inventors, Ts'ai Lun and Johann Gutenberg, make Hart's twenty *really* influential people. Other inventors who appear include James Watt, Orville and Wilbur Wright, Thomas Edison, Guglielmo Marconi, Alexander Graham Bell, Louis Daguerre, and Enrico Fermi. Hart's rationale for the ranking he assigns each inventor makes for enticing reading and should provoke not only insight on the part of students, but lively debate as well.

Regardless of whether teachers and students agree with Hart's ranking of the inventors named, familiarity with the inventors is requisite information for students. Many activities can grow from the initial catalyst *The 100* will provide. After students have researched and learned about the inventors Hart features, they can propose other inventors they believe should be included in an alternative list of 100 most influential people. A hall of fame panel can be set up and students can argue the case of their chosen inventor before their peers who have the authority to delete and add names to Hart's list or to create a completely new list. Students will not only acquire basic knowledge about inventors they study, they will develop and sharpen critical thinking skills in the process. Debates can be established to determine which inventor is the greatest inventor of all time. Is it Ts'ai Lun (the inventor of paper) as Hart suggests or someone else?

Debates can range beyond the contents of Hart's book. Students will develop and enhance research, critical thinking, and speaking skills when they debate such topics as:

Resolved: Necessity is the mother of invention.

Resolved: The computer is the most significant invention of the twentieth century.

Resolved: Invention flourishes most in times of war.

There should be both affirmative and negative positions, and the debaters should prepare briefs to support and substantiate their positions, anticipate counter arguments, and prepare possible rebuttals. It may be useful to ask students from high school debate teams to stage a sample debate and provide tips to the students about the processes of debate.

Round table discussions, less formal than debate, can also stimulate both thinking and research about the contributions of inventors and inventions. Each student can be asked to think about and defend his or her choice for the best invention of all time, the most remarkable or ingenious inventor, or the worst invention ever created.

INVENTION NEWSPAPERS

Students can create a newspaper about their studies of inventors, inventions, and the process of inventing. A lead story might relate to the inventors students have chosen as the most influential in history. A sample headline might read: Mrs. Johnson's Class Names Edison the Greatest Inventor in History. Editorial comments about the selection can also appear in the newspaper. News and feature stories about inventors and the creation of landmark inventions in history can be written. Students can draw advertisements for the newspaper to promote acceptance of their own inventions. Cartoons can be included as well as a comic strip about the continuing saga of a youthful inventor. Commentary on contemporary issues involving patents and trademarks could be included. Should the colorization of old black and white movies be allowed? Does an invention belong to the individual who creates it or to the company for which he or she works? Figure 2.5 is an example of a inventions newspaper front page.

INVENTION *Times*

BEAVERTAIL, UTAH   8-19-89   33¢

STUDENTS NAME EDISON GREATEST INVENTOR OF ALL TIME

(IP*) Duluth, MN

Students at Carmel Middle School have named Thomas Alva Edison the "World's Greatest Inventor." Edison beat out Ts'ai Lun, the Chinese inventor of paper, and Johann Gutenberg, the inventor of the printing press. James Watt and Alexander Graham Bell were next in order of importance in the poll of 200 students.

*Inventive Press

Book Review:

WOMEN CHEATED IN INVENTION HISTORIES, AUTHORS CLAIM

(IP)Los Angeles. Ethlie Ann Vare and Greg Ptacek have authored what may well be the first book ever devoted exclusively to women inventors. "The hand that rocks the cradle probably invented it, too" claims investigator Vare. Beginning with prehistory and the assertion that women in all probability were the inventors of agriculture, cooking, pottery, and other basic life activities, the authors trace the history of women inventors and discoverers into contemporary America. Among the accomplishments of women: the discovery of nuclear fission, invisible glass, pulsars, the Barbie Doll, ice cream cones, dress patterns, and radioactivity.

TEACHERS AND PARENTS NAME WORST INVENTIONS EVER

ALARM CLOCK BEATS OUT BOMBS!

(IP) Colorado Springs, CO.
More than 250 adults surveyed by students at Falcon High School in Colorado's Pikes Peak region named the alarm clock as humankind's worst invention. In fact, the morning bedroom fixture is so annoying that more adults listed it as the "worst thing ever invented" than even the atomic bomb. A majority of the respondents were school teachers or the parents of the students conducting the survey. Other items high on the annoyance scale for adults include: nuclear weapons, elevator music, dentist drills, "ghetto blaster" radios, and chewing gum. In response to the same question, middle and high school students named nuclear weapons and report cards as the least favored inventions.

Fig. 2.5. A sample invention newspaper.

INVENTION AS A MIRROR OF CIVILIZATION

The absolute and fundamental importance of invention to the history of civilization is beautifully articulated by James Burke in *Connections*,[6] which was the subject of a public television series. The singular quality which makes Burke's essays unique and of enormous value to gifted students is his weaving of the tapestry of civilization. He is not content to just describe a single invention and how it impacted the world. He takes the thread of an invention or event and traces it back through time to its origins. The connections he provides for readers on these journeys are illuminating. No student should begin a time line until he or she has read at least one of Burke's essays because time lines which are mere listings of dates in the evolution of technology offer no insight into cause and effect. As such, they are not only too simplistic for gifted learners, they are probably quite misleading as well. It is important for students to have a sense of the sweep and panorama of human history, but it is even more vital that they understand the interaction of all human events. Students must come to understand the whys as well as be able to recite the whats, whens, and wheres.

Two examples of the richness of provocative reading and thinking *Connections* offer are found in Burke's discussion of the inventions of warfare and his thoughts on China's contributions to inventions. In a chapter called "Distant Voices," he begins by surveying the impact of Enrico Fermi's contributions to the development of the atomic bomb, but quickly transports readers back to the European Middle Ages. Burke recounts how a single invention, the saddle stirrup, allowed the Norman troops of William the Conqueror to triumph over the Saxons at the Battle of Hastings in 1066, forever changing the history and the language of the British people. In yet another excellent exposition, Burke offers an explanation about the import *and* restraints upon Chinese invention:

That the Chinese discovered gunpowder is not in doubt. What *is* in question is whether or not they used it the same way as the Europeans did. Perhaps the entire question of Chinese invention is worth a brief digression at this point. The major inventions attributed with certainty to the Chinese include paper, silk weaving, clockwork, astronomical instruments, the horizontal loom, the spinning wheel and the waterwheel. These are inventions fundamental in the history of man as a tool-maker. The medieval Chinese were without doubt the most fruitfully inventive people on Earth. However, the fact that the technology of the modern world is Western shows to what extent the two cultures were different at a time vital in the history of the effects of innovation on society. In the stable, civilized East the innovations were not permitted to bring about radical social changes as they were in the brawling, dynamic West. The chief reason for this may have been the stultifying effects of Chinese bureaucracy, which owed its origins to the geographical nature of the country. China is a land of wide plains and major rivers. Early in recorded history the Chinese undertook vast irrigation schemes, and the scale on which manpower for these projcts was mobilized demanded firm, centralized planning and control. The civil service which evolved to run the irrigation schemes was to remain in power for thousands of years, guarding its position and privilege against change, maintaining a society rigidly stratified into classes between which movement was virtually impossible. There was no drive for the individual to use technology to improve his lot and so rise in the world, because rising in the world was out of the question. Thus it was that invention may have come from the East, but it was only in the West that it brought widespread change. To oversimplify the case: in China gunpowder propelled arrows, and even exploded grenades; in the West it destroyed cities.*

---

*From *Connections* by James Burke, © 1978. By permission of Little, Brown and Company.

HISTORY: WHERE DO INVENTIONS COME FROM?

As Burke suggests, the Chinese may have been the most fruitfully creative and inventive people in the history of civilization. He cites as evidence their invention of paper, clockworks, the spinning wheel, and astronomical instruments. Figure 2.6 shows the Chinese characters for the concept of invention. The top character, "Fa," means to grow, burst forth, or discover. "Ming" represents sunshine, brightness, insight, and understanding.

Fig. 2.6. Chinese characters which taken together express the concept "invention." Calligraphy by Tina Cheng.

Ask students to choose a country, determine its national language, and discover its word for invention. Next ask students to research and identify the major inventions by the peoples of their chosen nation. Finally, ask students to list and mark significant landmarks in their chosen country's invention history on the classroom time line. Students should be able to locate much of this information in the LMC with the assistance of the library media specialist.

WOMEN INVENTORS

What do the plane astrolab, the Geiger counter, the cotton gin, chocolate chip cookies, nuclear fission, Liquid Paper, Glo-Sheets, and the Katalavox all have in common? Women, singly or in collaboration with others, either invented, discovered, or participated in the development of these things. Women inventors go back at least as far as Hypatia of Alexandria (b. 370 A.D.), who invented the plane astrolab and the hydroscope, but was executed by fanatics when she wrote about equal rights for women. The cotton gin, though credited to patent holder Eli Whitney, was probably invented by his landlady, Catherine Greene. Though she never patented her work, Marie Curie discovered radioactivity and invented what is now known as the Geiger counter. A 1939 scientific article by German scientist Dr. Lise Meitner first calculated the possibilities of nuclear fission. Of Jewish birth, she had fled Nazi Germany and was working in a laboratory in Sweden at the time. Ruth Wakefield invented the chocolate chip cookie. Bette Nesmith Graham invented Liquid Paper to cover up mistakes she made as a typist in a bank in Dallas, Texas. Martine Kempf was a young astronomy student when she began to develop the Katalavox, the computer system which allows physically disabled persons to operate wheelchairs and delicate equipment like microscopes with voice commands. Becky Schroeder invented Glo-Sheets when she was ten and by age twelve held the patent for the special writing surface which allows police and doctors to write in relative darkness.

In past centuries, women have been denied educational and work opportunities which often serve as prerequisites of invention. Societal attitudes certainly contributed to the notion that invention was men's work. Even when women did invent something, they often had to let their husbands or other men apply for the patents because they were not allowed to own property. Tragically, black women were in an even worse dilemma. For example, Ellen Eglui, inventor of the clothes wringer in the 1880s, virtually gave her invention away because she believed white women would not use something created by a black woman.

For much of history, the contributions of women to the history of invention have been obscured. Two authors, Ethlie Ann Vare and Greg Ptacek, have set out to set the record straight. *Mothers of Invention: From the Bra to the Bomb: Forgotten Women & Their Unforgettable Inventions* is a timely book which goes a long way toward rectifying the dismal treatment of women in invention literature.

The authors begin with a discussion of fundamental inventions such as weaving, cooking, pottery, and the cultivation of crops which were probably invented by women. They move through antiquity into modern times naming and discussing the many unsung accomplishments of women inventors and discoverers. The accounts in the book are interesting and informative. Most of the stories are relatively short which make them highly suitable for reading to the entire class. The women and their inventions examined in *Mothers of Invention* include:

Anna Bissell — carpet sweeper

Melitta Bentz — coffee pot

Sirvart A. Mellian — contoured protective body armor

Amanda Jones — vacuum canning

Rose O'Neill — Kewpie Doll

Ruth Handler — Barbie Doll

Anna Kalso — Earth Shoe

Lillian Russell — dresser-trunk

Carrie J. Everson — ore extraction process[7]

One myth which may need to be explored is that when women do invent, they invent only domestic appliances and tools. In an excellent article in *New Scientist*, University of Minnesota professor Fred Amram notes that during World War I women received patents for the following inventions:

percussion and ignition fuse

railway torpedo

rear sight for guns

submarine mine

torpedo guard

incendiary ball

cane-gun

bomb-launching apparatus

automatic pistol[8]

The Amran article and Vare and Ptacek book both note that Martha Coston invented the signal flare first used by the U.S. government during the Civil War. Following the war, she patented and marketed her flares, which were used by ships at sea and throughout Europe. More recently, Marguerite Shue-wen Chang patented a trigger device for setting off an underground nuclear explosive.[9]

The role of women inventors is only very recently receiving the attention it deserves. In 1988, the Goldstein Gallery at the University of Minnesota staged an exhibition of inventions by women in a show entitled "Her Works Praise Her." The recent flowering of invention contests in schools across the United States will hopefully serve as a catalyst to inspire more research and publication of past and present efforts of women inventors.

Many fine projects can stem from investigations of women inventors. Organizations such as the National Women's History Project (P.O. Box 3716, Santa Rosa, California 95402) and local women's study and historical society organizations may be able to direct students to further information and resources regarding accomplishments of past women inventors. Students may want to contact invention organizations listed in the resources section of this text with similar inquiries, or to network with contemporary women inventors. Students might also contact the research and development sections of local corporations to determine if there are women engineers and scientists employed there who would share some of their experiences and work with innovation, discovery, and invention with the class.

An annual calendar celebrating the accomplishments of women in science and technology is published and sold by the Detroit Area Chapter of the Association for Women in Science. (For information, contact Women in Science calendar, The Association for Women in Science, Detroit Area Chapter, P.O. Box 721072S, Berkley, Michigan 48072.) The Women's Bureau of the U.S. Department of Labor (200 Constitution Avenue, N.W., Washington, D.C. 20210), and the Society of Women Engineers (345 East 47th Street, Room 305, New York, New York 10017) might also be useful sources for students to check.

In Canada, the Women's Inventors Project (WIP) is a nonprofit organization which encourages and provides assistance to women inventors. The WIP publishes a newsletter, provides workshops for both women and school-age girls on the subject of inventing, and has published two books, *The Book for Women Who Invent or Want To* (1986) and *Daughters of Invention: An Invention Workshop for Girls* (1988). For further information, contact Marie Le Lievre, Women Inventors Project, 22 King Street South, Suite 500, Waterloo, Ontario N2J 1N8.

Projects for students studying women as inventors could include:

time lines of women's contribution to inventions

profile and fact sheets about women inventors

a paper or speech about the many prejudices and legal hurdles women have had to overcome in order to invent and receive patents

a catalog of drawings of inventions created by women

a hall of fame learning center devoted to women inventors

a dramatic recreation of an important episode or event in the life of one of history's accomplished women inventors

a "women only" invention convention

WRITING ABOUT INVENTORS

One of the axioms in the field of education for the gifted is that it is important these students be producers rather than mere consumers of information. Joseph S. Renzulli is one of many experts in the field of gifted education who emphasizes the importance of having gifted students create products which can be shared with significant audiences.[10] One way gifted students can share their research of the lives of inventors is through the creation of books for younger readers. "Henry and Me" (see figure 2.7) is an example of such an effort. The sixth-grade author uses a style of fictional biography first popularized by Robert Lawson in *Ben and Me,* in which a mouse recounts the life of Benjamin Franklin. More recently Robert Quackenbush has authored a series of biographies of famous inventors such as Alexander Graham Bell, Charles Goodyear, and Samuel F. B. Morse for young readers. "Henry and Me" uses a personable lizard to relate instances of importance in the life of automobile inventor Henry Ford.

One of the complaints of elementary teachers is that there are too few creative and good biographies about inventors for their students to read. Gifted middle and high school students can help alleviate this problem while simultaneously developing their own talents. There are at least two approaches to this activity. Students can select an inventor of note, research his or her life, and write a general biography for children. The completed books can then be given to elementary LMCs. Another approach involves more effort, but may provide a richer payoff for all concerned. Have a secondary class "adopt" an elementary school class. Pair older students and younger students during a get acquainted session. The task of the older student is to find out what his younger partner knows about inventors, the name of his or her favorite inventor or invention, and some general information about his or her life. After the initial get together, the older students research the inventors of choice and write and illustrate a book about the life of the inventor the child has named. At an appropriate date, the older students present the gift biographies to their younger, "adopted" brothers and sisters. A variation on the latter theme would be to have each student create a biography about an inventor for a younger sibling, cousin, or neighbor. If the school has a sister city school in another country, consider replicating this project long distance. Do not let language be a barrier. If translations are needed, enlist the support of the foreign language department and add a whole new learning dimension to the project. Duplicate copies of the final products can be housed in the LMC as part of the biography collection.

Henry and Me
The proper story of Henry Ford and his lizard, Clyde.

I was riding in my car made of an empty matchbox, toothpicks and cardboard wheels. My car rolled to a stop after coasting down a small hill. Quickly, I got out of my small car. I wasn't watching where I was walking and ran into a cat. Suddenly, I turned around and started running as fast as my small legs would carry me. When I stopped running, I found that I was in some sort of building. I heard a man working on some weird-looking object. Pretty soon, I saw a man in blue pants and a red shirt. I had seen him before pictured on an old scrap of newspaper.

"It must be Henry Ford," I said to myself.

There was a piece of string dangling from his work table. I grabbed the string and climbed up it. When I reached the top, I crawled up on the table and said, "Are you Henry Ford?"

He looked down and said, "Yes, but you can just call me Henry."

"Oh, and call me Clyde," I said. He told me all about his engine and told me to go inside it and connect two wires that were loose. I crawled inside, being careful not to scratch myself on many sharp parts. When I found the wires, I connected them. To my surprise, the engine started. Henry had forgotten to turn the power off before I got in. The pistons kept hitting my head every time they came down. Finally, I found a way out. I had a terrible headache and was covered completely with oil. Henry went into the kitchen and brought back a dish of water, a small sliver of soap and a piece of a rag. I washed myself thoroughly, and got out. I found a small piece of a pencil and started to draw a car.

When I finished I said, "This car is lightweight and is cheap enough for everyone to have one."

He looked at my drawing and then said, "It's a good idea, but how does it run?"

I looked at him. "Your engine," I said.

He went out of the room and came back with boards, nails, screws, tools and everything he needed. When he got back, he started building. When he finished his car, it looked like a cross between a farm wagon and a giant propeller.

I looked at it carefully and said, "It won't sell."

Henry looked at me with a puzzled look and said, "Why not?"

"It's going to be harder than I thought," I said to myself. "First," I said, "You have to take off that silly looking propeller and hook up a drive shaft." I drew him a picture. "Then, you have to change the shape of the car ... the wheels should be sturdy, you need a steering wheel, seats, and safety devices." I showed him how to make brakes, a steering wheel, a gas pedal and headlights and tail lights.

After a few days, he finished his car. Outside his workshop he hung a sign that said:

1892 Ford Motor Car
Two Cylinder
Four horse power $200 each

The years went by with Henry making cars. One day I said, "Henry, you need more speed."

"You're right Clyde," he said.

(Fig. 2.7 continues on page 36.)

Fig. 2.7—Continued

After a few years, he had another sign out which said:
  1903 Ford Model 999
  1903 Ford Arrow
  1908 Ford Model T
  All with four cylinders, 80 horse power engines,
  $300 each
His employees were complaining of having only $5.00 for an 8-hour day. I told Henry that he should raise their salary. He raised it to $6.00 a day. Soon, he moved and started his own factory. 1928 rolled along and Henry, with my help, changed his cars in design and construction. He also started building lightweight farm tractors. One day, a screw was loose inside his tractor engine. Before I got in, I asked Henry if the engine's power was off. I crawled in and tightened the screw as best I could. Henry and I had many happy years together until he died in 1945.

Fig. 2.7. "Henry and Me," by Greg Haynes, sixth grade student at the Colorado Springs (Colorado) Christian School. Used with permission. Illustration by Adam Burton.

INVENTION SURVEYS

Students can practice many research techniques as part of their learning about inventions and inventors. They can take a poll to determine how knowledgeable average citizens are about inventions by asking them to match famous inventors with their inventions. They can ask people to name the invention they believe to be the most important of all time. They can even ask people to name the invention they wish *had not* been invented. The author had fun asking people representative of several age and professional groups to name the top ten most vexing inventions of all time. A sampling of the results follows:

child-proof aspirin bottles (which only children can open)

car horns

Susan B. Anthony dollars

vending machines which take your money, but do not deliver the promised candy, pop, etc.

watches that beep

telephone answering machines

assembly instructions for toys which cannot be deciphered

mini inflatable spare tires which now come as standard equipment

automatic teller machines

easy-open boxes which are not

talking automobile reminders (e.g., "Your headlights are on.")

sporks (plastic fork/spoon combination utensil)

elevator music

Students can tabulate and graph results and share the results of their survey through their own invention newspaper or submit their results to the local newspapers and television stations.

This learning experiment may be a quick, fun, and largely informal task, or it may be developed into a sophisticated lesson about sampling and survey research in which subject selection, procedures, and statistical analysis are vital parts of the learning experience.

THE INVENTION OF ORDINARY THINGS

Our association with the artifacts of modern life is so commonplace and pervasive that we tend to assume they have always been around. But we have not always had telephones, airplanes, automobiles, and television, or for that matter Band-Aids, Dixie Cups, or Kleenex. Where did all these things we take for granted come from? People had to *invent* these items and thousand more like them. One class participation exercise which allows for considerable sharing of research and findings is to assign each student the task of researching a common, everyday item to determine its invention and usage history. Many sources, including encyclopedias, are useful for this task. Five especially good texts are:

Caney, Steven. *Steven Caney's Invention Book*. New York: Workman Publishing Company, Inc., 1985.

de Bono, Edward. *Eureka! An Illustrated History of Inventions from the Wheel to the Computer*. New York: Holt, Rinehart and Winston, 1974.

Hooper, Meredith. *Everyday Inventions*. New York: Taplinger Publishing Company, 1976.

Panati, Charles. *Extraordinary Origins of Everyday Things*. New York: Harper & Row, 1987.

Wulffson, Don L. *The Invention of Ordinary Things*. New York: Lothrop, Lee, & Shepard Books, 1981.

Items which are chronicled in these books include the following inventions which may serve as an excellent class research list:

shopping cart	bicycle
shoes	rubber band
toothbrush	traffic light
alarm clock	soap
chewing gum	Christmas card
vacuum cleaner	lock and key
barbed wire	sewing machine
typewriter	ball-point pen
razor	false teeth
umbrellas	zipper
earmuffs	water skis
Kleenex	Frisbee
milk bottle	roller skates
tea bag	Life Savers candy

Each of the suggested texts has a relatively short history of these and many more commonplace items. The selections are short, yet highly interesting accounts which are great for oral reading at the beginning or end of class sessions.

Students can present their individual findings about assigned commonplace inventions in many diverse and creative ways. Oral reports are one obvious way, but students might also dress as the inventor and dramatically recreate the invention of their particular item. The "You Are There" format works well to recreate through drama great moments in invention history. Posters and comic books can also artistically and persuasively tell about the invention of a common item. Creative students will no doubt think of many other alternatives.

THE *SEARS, ROEBUCK & CO. CATALOG* AS A MIRROR OF THE TIMES

At the turn of the century, the *Sears, Roebuck & Co. Catalog* was in many ways a mirror of the times, especially with respect to the inventions which impacted the daily living of ordinary citizens. Fig. 2.8 is a sample page from the 1908 catalog. Ask students to note the invention represented on this page and how it may have affected the lives of people who used it. Facsimile copies of many past Sears, Roebuck & Co. catalog can be obtained from school and local libraries. Ask students to peruse such catalogs and note the changes wrought by the proliferation of new inventions in the marketplace. Take the assignment further by having students compare today's Sears catalog with one from the past. A comparison of the appliances and tools utilized in the preparation and preservation of food, for example, between 1908 and 1988 will be most revealing. Remind students that the 1908 items were used by their great grandparents. Old catalogs are windows into the everyday life the way it was lived in generations past.

Fig. 2.8. Who needs stereo? As long as your parlor boasts an Oxford Cylinder Talking Machine—as illustrated in the 1908 Sears, Roebuck & Co. catalog—you could enjoy the "most natural and beautiful tone" a flower horn machine ever produced! Courtesy Sears Archives.

INSIDE THE MIND OF AN INVENTOR

Thomas Alva Edison is generally acknowledged as the most famous inventor of all time. During his lifetime he secured 1,093 patents. His list of inventions include incandescent and fluorescent lamps, the phonograph, and the motion picture camera and projector. Edison was famous not only for his inventions, but for his work habits. His industriousness was legend. He worked amazingly long hours, purportedly begrudging the need for sleep. Today, he might be called a workaholic.

In the summer of 1885, following a year of mourning for his first wife who died of typhoid fever, Edison took one of the few sustained vacations in his life. During this tranquil summer, Edison read leisurely, courted his soon-to-be new wife, Mina Miller, and paid an extended visit to friends in the seaside town of Winthrop, Massachusetts, north of Boston. An interesting mark of Edison's highly original mind and his diversity of skills is the fact that he proposed to Mina Miller on board a passenger train by tapping into her palm in Morse Code his proposal of marriage. Miss Miller, to whom Edison had taught Morse Code, responded in kind, "Yes." While spending lazy days in Winthrop and elsewhere, Edison penned the only diary he was ever known to keep. Figure 2.9 is a reproduction of a page from Edison's diary. Figure 2.10 is the partial text of the very first entry in Edison's diary.[11]

Students should note the wit and humor Edison displays as well as the allusions he makes. To fully appreciate Edison's diary entry, students may need to research the references to Havana, dyspepsia, metaphysics, and Plato. Not only is the entry a revelation of the playfulness of Edison's mind, it is also an indication of his familiarity with great writers and thinkers.

Menlo Park 11 ♀

Sunday July 12 1885

Awakened at 5.15 AM. my eyes were embarassed by the sunbeams - turned my back to them and tried to take another dip into oblivion - suceeded - awakened at 7 AM. thought of Mina Daisy. and Mamma G— put all 3 in my mental kaledescope to obtain a new combination a la Galton. took Mina as a basis, tried to improve her beauty by discarding and adding certain features borrowed from Daisy and Mamma G. a sort of Raphaelized beauty, got into it too deep, mind flew away and I went to sleep again. Awakened at 8 15 AM. Poweful itching of my head, lots of white dry dandruff— what is this d——mnable material, Perhaps its the dust from the dry literary matter I've crowded into my noddle lately Its nomadic. gets all over my coat, must read about it in the Encyclopedia, Smoking too much makes me nervous — must lasso my natural tendency to acquire such habits — holding heavy cigar constantly in my mouth has deformed my upper lip, it has a sort of Havanna curl. Arose at 9 oclock came down stairs expecting twas too late for breakfast—twasn't. couldn't eat much, nerves of stomach too Nicotinny. The roots of tobacco plants must go clear through to hell. Satans principal agent Dyspepsia

Fig. 2.9. A page from Thomas Edison's diary. Courtesy of U.S. Department of the Interior, National Park Service, Edison National Historic Site.

Menlo Park N.Y.
Sunday July 12, 1885

Awakened at 5:15 a.m. My eyes were embarassed [sic] by the sunbeams — turned my back to them and tried to take another dip into oblivion — succeeded. Awakened at 8:15 a.m. Powerful itching of my head, lots of white dry dandruff — what is this d---mnable material, Perhaps its the dust from the dry literary matter I've crowded into my noddle [sic] lately ... Its nomadic. Gets all over my coat, must read about it in the Encyclopedia. Smoking too much makes me nervous — must lasso my natural tendency to acquire such habits — holding heavy cigar constantly in my mouth has deformed my upper lip, it has a sort of Havanna [sic] curl. Arose at 9 oclock came down stairs expecting twas too late for breakfast — twasn't. couldn't eat much, nerves of stomach too nicotinny. The roots of tobacco plants must go clear through to hell. Satan's principal agent Dyspepsia must have charge of this branch of the vegitable [sic] kingdom. — It has just occured [sic] to me that the grain may digest certain portions of food, say the etherial part, as well as the stomach — perhaps dandruff is the excreta of the mind — the quantity of this material being directly proportional to the amount of reading one indulges in. A book on German metaphysics would thus easily ruin a dress suit. — I think freckles on the skin are due to some salt of Iron, sunlight brings them out by reducing them from high to low state of oxidation — perhaps with a powerful magnet applied for some time, and then with proper chemicals, these mudholes of beauty might be removed. *Dot is very [sic] busy cleaning the abode of our deaf and dumb parrot — she has fed it tons of edibles and never got a sound out of it. This bird has the taciturnity of a statue, and the dirt producing capacity of a drove of buffalo. This is by far the nicest day of this season, neither too hot or too cold. — it blooms on the apex of perfection — an Edenday Good day for an angels pic nic [sic]. They could lunch on the smell of flowers and new mown hay, drink the moisture of the air, and dance to the hum of bees. Fancy the Soul of Plato astride of a butterfly riding around Menlo Park with a lunch basket.

*Nickname of Marion, Edison's daughter and eldest child.

Fig. 2.10. Partial text from Edison's first diary entry.

BIOGRAPHIES OF INVENTORS

A natural extension of reading Edison's diary entry would be to read a biography of this great inventor. A peek into Edison's life may also inspire students to want to learn more about one of the many other famous inventors. Because gifted students are typically omnivorous readers, it should not be difficult to engage them in the reading of biographies of inventors. Since biographers have found inventors to be vital subjects, there is not a paucity of biographies about inventors, although there clearly is a dearth of works about women inventors. Becky Schroeder, Sister Tabith Babbit, and Margaret Bailey are three women inventors mentioned in literature about inventors, but biographies of women inventors, with the exception of Marie Curie, appear to be all but nonexistent at the present time. Students also need to be cautioned that not all biographies are of equal merit. The library media specialist can be an especially valuable ally in locating and directing gifted students to choice biographies of inventors. A discussion of the responsibilities of a biographer and the merits of good biography may well be in order prior to assigning students the task of reading biographies about inventors.

The following list of inventors and discoverers is by no means all inclusive, but it should serve as an introductory guide for students in selecting biographies.

Archimedes	King Camp Gillette
Charles Babbage	Robert Goddard
Alexander Graham Bell	Johannes Gutenberg
Henry Bessemer	Edwin Land
Louis Braille	Antoine van Leeuwenhoek
Werner von Braun	Guglielmo Marconi
Jacques-Yves Cousteau	Jacques and Joseph Montgolfier
Marie Curie	Samuel Morse
Louis Daguerre	Alfred Nobel
Gottlieb Wilhelm Daimler	Louis Pasteur
George Eastman	Nikola Tesla
Thomas Edison	Charles Townes
Michael Faraday	Leonardo da Vinci
Enrico Fermi	James Watt
Henry Ford	Eli Whitney
Benjamin Franklin	Orville and Wilbur Wright
R. Buckminster Fuller	Vladimir Kosma Zworykin
Galileo Galilei	

When multiple biographies are available, as in the case of Edison, Franklin, Curie, and the Wright brothers, it may be useful to have students work in pairs or small groups to compare and critique the biographies read. In all cases, students should examine biographies for accuracy, completeness of the treatment of the subject, use of primary and secondary sources, and fairness of the portrait. Figure 2.11 may serve as an entry-level critique sheet. The worksheets can be compiled alphabetically by subjects' names for future reference by other students searching for good biographies.

BIOGRAPHY REPORT FORM

Title _____

Author _____

Publisher _____

Date of Publication _____ No. Pages _____

Circle the features included in this biography:

Index   Illustrations   Appendix   Bibliography

A. Indicate what portions of the subject's life are examined in this biography.

B. Is the overall impression of the subject yielded positive, negative, or neutral?

C. Does the biographer appear to present a balanced portrait of the subject and his/her contributions?

D. What new things did you learn about the subject from the biography?

E. What is the greatest strength or value of this work?

F. What is the greatest weakness or limitation of this work?

Please comment on other aspects of this biography which should be further considered by prospective readers.

Fig. 2.11. Sample format for a critique sheet.

Biographies can be illuminating, insightful, and inspiring. A good biographer provides adequate background information so that contemporary readers not only learn about the subject but about the times in which he or she lived. Good biographies go beyond simple descriptions of highlights in an inventor's life; they reveal the roles hard work and chance played in the life of an inventor. They may reveal something about perseverance, which, if not a universal trait among inventors, has nevertheless served some like Edison well. Sidney Parnes shares one story about Edison which illumines this point.

> Thomas Edison was known as a tireless opportunity-maker. After thousands of unsuccessful experiments on one of his projects, a discouraged assistant complained that they had achieved no results. "No results!" exclaimed Edison. "We've had wonderful results! We already know thousands of things that won't work."[12]

In a contemporary society which places such a high premium on being first and has taught young people to look at mistakes as failures rather than opportunities for new learning experiences, Edison's words can be truly inspiring.

Rarely were the lives of any inventors unqualified successes. Goodyear, for example, suffered defeat after defeat, public ridicule, and even spent time in debtor's prison, yet refused to give up his pursuit of inventing a method for the vulcanization of rubber. Young people have too often grown up associating giants of invention like Goodyear, the Wright brothers, Edison, and Marie Curie with their final and miraculous inventions or the Nobel Prizes won *without* the realization that years of sacrifice, failure, and hard work were required for such achievements. Biographies illuminate the invention and discovery processes when they tell the whole story behind the achievements of notable peoples.

Exceptional biographies are not only instructive as to the lives of the subjects, but may describe in detail the actual experiments and processes utilized by the inventors in their endeavors. When this occurs, a whole new dimension to the learning experience may be added. Using such biographies as a guide, enterprising students may actually replicate the experiments conducted first by the famous subjects.

Many possible products can result from the reading of biographies. Several of the most famous inventors are contemporaries, so a round table discussion, like Steve Allen's "Meeting Of The Minds," where students portray the subject about whom they have read may be highly effective. Staying in character, students could, for example, create a scene in which Thomas Edison, Henry Ford, and Alexander Graham Bell discuss their respective inventions as well as affairs of the world.

Figure 2.12 suggests further ideas for product development by students as extensions of their reading of biographies. The instructions are written directly for students for ease of use by teachers.

Figure 2.13 is an example of an acrostic poem a student might write after reading a book or article about the life of Edison. It represents yet another use of information gleaned from reading biographies.

Figure 2.14 (page 49) is a profile of inventor Nikola Tesla which may be shared with students.

(Text continues on page 51.)

INVENTION BIOGRAPHY PROJECT IDEAS

1. Write a letter to the subject of the biography you read, and describe the impact his or her invention still has on life in the world today.

2. Write a profile of the inventor whose biography you have read for inclusion in the *INVENTION TIMES* newspaper.

3. Use an artistic format of your choice, and contribute to the classroom bulletin board, "Gallery of Famous Inventors," information about the inventor whose biography you have read.

4. Select a well-known central event in an inventor's life and compare several accounts of the same happening found in other biographies of the inventor's life.

5. Write a diary entry the inventor you have read about might have kept.

6. Remain in the character of the subject and write a letter to another famous inventor describing your latest work. For example, if you are Nikola Tesla, write to Thomas Edison and tell him about your experiments with dynamos.

7. Create a resumé or a job description for the subject of the biography you have read. Use only facts and information you have learned from reading the biography.

8. Prepare a scrapbook of drawings, newspaper clippings, handwritten notes, etc. (all of which you create) which figure prominently in the life of the inventor whose biography you have read.

9. Create a time line of the inventor's life which depicts not only the high points in his or her life, but which also notes the inventor's contemporaries and significant events which occurred in the subject's life span.

10. Imagine you are a young, eager reporter for the *INVENTION TIMES*, and you have been given the task of interviewing the famous inventor who is the subject of the biography you have read. Create a list of 10 questions you want to ask the famous inventor. Provide hypothetical answers to the questions.

11. Create a passport for the inventor about whom you have read. What interesting places and locales figure in his or her life?

12. Create a cartoon or drawing which depicts the famous inventor you have read about at the magic moment of his or her greatest triumph.

Fig. 2.12. Student handout.

T ROUBLED YOUTH

SPENT H OURS IN CHILDHOOD LAB

O HIO BORN

M OTION PICTURE CREATOR

A CERBIC WIT

HIS FATHER, S AM EDISON

A

L

V

A

E

D

I

S

O

N

Fig. 2.13. An acrostic on the subject Thomas Alva Edison.

An Inventor Profile: Nikola Tesla

His biographers argue that Nikola Tesla was the most brilliant inventor who ever lived. Proponents of Tesla's genius claim that his talent was of such proportion that he was the one famous inventor of his time—which includes giants like Edison—who could come back today and not be surprised at the scientific developments he would observe. Indeed, some of Tesla's documented experiments cannot be duplicated today, almost a century after they were first completed. One nuclear engineer has even suggested that Russian scientists have secretly developed force fields of offensive and defensive weapons based upon theories proposed by Tesla nearly a century ago. Who was this man who is not found in history books along side contemporary inventors such as Edison and the Wright brothers, yet is so highly praised?

Nikola Tesla was born the son of a Serbian Orthodox clergyman in 1856 in a part of Austria-Hungary which is present-day Yugoslavia. Ironically, it was an older brother, Daniel, who gave every appearance of being the family prodigy and was expected to be a great scholar. Tragically, this youth died in a childhood accident. In the tradition-bound Europe of the 19th century, the surviving son was expected to follow his father into the clergy, but young Nikola Tesla's brilliance and heart lay in the direction of science. His father yielded and Tesla entered the Austrian Polytechnical School in Graz in 1875. He later studied at the University of Prague. In 1882, he began work at the Continental Edison Company in Paris. However, the real activity in electrical engineering was occurring in the United States, so Tesla moved to New York in 1884.

For a brief time, Tesla worked directly for Edison. It was not a happy match. Edison and Tesla possessed egos and eccentricities which clashed. In addition to quarreling over invention rights and money, the two were the fathers of the two competing means of transmitting electrical current. Tesla invented alternating current and the machinery to make it practical. Edison was the chief proponent of direct current. Though Edison was by far the more successful inventor and businessman, Tesla's alternating current, backed chiefly by George Westinghouse, prevailed and won the usage war of the currents. Tesla's discoveries and inventions related to alternating current made possible for the first time the generation of electricity at one locale and its subsequent transmission to distant areas. His efforts led to harnessing the power of Niagara Falls in 1895 and the conversion and transmission of that energy to create electric lighting in cities miles away.

In addition to developing alternating current, Tesla is often credited as the true inventor of radio, neon and fluorescent lighting, and high frequency induction heating. He accurately forecasted radar and, in 1898, developed radio-guided torpedoes. He developed the Tesla coil which is an air core transformer that transforms low voltages into very high voltages. In 1900, in Colorado Springs, Colorado, he built the world's largest Tesla coil which produced electrical sparks up to 135 feet in length. With his experiments, he produced both lightning and an earthquake.

(Fig. 2.14 continues on page 50.)

Fig. 2.14 — *Continued*

He counted Mark Twain among his friends and he dazzled New York City's high society with his electrical experiments. At the turn of the century, he was probably as famous as Edison. So why is so little known of him today? He was probably his own worst enemy. An extremely eccentric man, Tesla did not bother to patent many of his inventions. As a result, his financial fortunes fluctuated wildly throughout his adult life. When he did work with others, he moved quickly from one flash of genius to another, leaving others to do the slow and painstaking research and development essential in science. Unlike Edison, who employed armies of engineers to assist with his experiments and bring theoretical ideas to fruition as practical realities, Tesla chiefly worked alone. Supposedly blessed with a photographic memory, Tesla kept only sporadic notes about his many theories, experiments, and inventions. He became more and more eccentric and isolated in his later years, confiding his ideas and knowledge to no one. He never married and when he died in 1943, there were no heirs or supportive colleagues to promote his place in invention history. Only in more recent years have biographers began to urge a reexamination of Tesla's genius and his contributions to science.

Students who wish to know more about Nikola Tesla's life and works may consult these resources:

Cheney, Margaret. *Tesla: Man Out of Time.* Englewood Cliffs, N.J.: Prentice-Hall, Inc., 1981.

Hunt, Inez, and Wanetta Draper. *Lightning in His Hand: The Life Story of Nikola Tesla.* Hawthorne, Calif.: Omni Publications, 1977.

Students may also be interested to know that there is a contemporary organization of scientists that continue to study and honor Tesla's accomplishments. The International Tesla Society, Inc. is located at 330 A West Uintah Street, Suite 215, Colorado Springs, CO 80905-1095 (also at High Energy Enterprises, P.O. Box 5636, Security, CO 80931). The society sponsors an annual Tesla conference which draws researchers and historians from around the globe.

Fig. 2.14. A sample biographical profile.

TIME LINES

Time lines can be very effective in assisting students to visualize the accomplishments of inventors as well as provide them with a sense of history. A time line which examines accomplishments across many fields will dramatically illustrate just how far ahead of their time many inventors were. Contemporaries of Edison publicly claimed that the incandescent lamp was a practical impossibility. A time line may reveal a sudden burst and flurry of activity in a particular field at one certain period in history. Certainly the development of nuclear energy and of nuclear weapons was directly related to the Allied war efforts in World War II. Time lines may reveal the dependence one field of inventive activity had upon a second field of invention. For example, automobiles and airplanes were dependent upon the development of various kinds of engines.

Time lines should be a feature of any classroom seriously studying inventions and inventing as they provide a visual context into which students can continually fit newly acquired information. There are, of course, commercially produced time lines. However, the most instructive time lines will most likely be ones created by the students themselves. There are a variety of types. Students might create a time line of the inventions of just one nation, or parallel time lines showing the progress of inventing in several countries. Time lines can be in a broad field such as aviation, or relate to a single object like the phonograph. A time line might be created to reveal the history of inventions related to special segments of the population. The invention of Braille and electric wheel chairs could appear on a time line of inventions designed to assist people with handicaps or impairments. Yet another specialized time line might show the development of children's toys. A time line might reveal the chronology of the inventions of a single genius like Edison. Myriad other possibilities exist. The important thing is for students to glimpse at least a part of the grand panorama that is history and to understand the critical role invention has played in the creation of that history.

Figure 2.15 is one example of a possible time line formatting which may be shared with students.

Several excellent resources exist to assist students. These include books specific to invention as well as more general resources:

Giscard d'Estaing, Valerie-Anne. *The World Almanac Book of Inventions.* New York: World Almanac Publications, 1985.

Chiefly an encyclopedia of inventions and inventing, this work and its sequel, *The Second World Almanac Book of Inventions* (1986), outline the history of thousands of inventions in dozens of fields. The first volume contains information and dates about developments in the fields of transportation, armaments, agriculture, the arts, media and communications, games, toys and sports, everyday life, medicine, science, energy, information systems, and industry. In each section the story of invention is told chronologically, which makes the construction of time lines considerably easier.

Grun, Bernard. *The Timetables of History: A Horizontal Linkage of People and Events.* New York: Simon and Schuster, 1982.

This massive text lists major events and happenings from 5000 B.C. through A.D. 1978 across the fields of history and politics, literature, religion and philosophy, visual arts, music, science, technology, and growth, and daily life.

LANDMARKS IN AVIATION HISTORY

1896   Englishman J. Challis coins the word "airplane"

1903   Wright Brothers experience first powered, controlled, sustained flight in an airplane

1909   Frenchman Henri Fabre invents the seaplane, "Hydravion"

1915   German Fokkers equipped with firing guns

1924   German Junker trimotor aircraft built

1935   Boeing demonstrates B-17 bomber

1936   Douglas DC-3 passenger aircraft built

1939   von Ohain builds first jet craft, "Heinkel He 178"

1942   First U.S. jet flight, "X-59"

1944   Messerschmitt and Gloster Meteor are first jet fighters

1947   USA, Bell "X-1", first airplane to exceed speed of sound

       "B-47" bomber produced

1949   De Havilland "Comet," first jet passenger plane to fly

1953   Pratt and Whitney supersonic combat fighter

1959   U.S. "X-15" rocket-powered plane

1960   "Hawker Harrier" vertical-take-off jet tested

1969   "Concorde" supersonic airliner makes maiden flight

1970   Boeing 747 "Jumbo Jets" begin service

1977   U.S. Space Shuttle first tested

1980   American Paul McCready invents solar aircraft, "Gossamer Penguin"

1986   "Voyager" built. Jeana Yeager and Richard Butan fly around the world without refueling

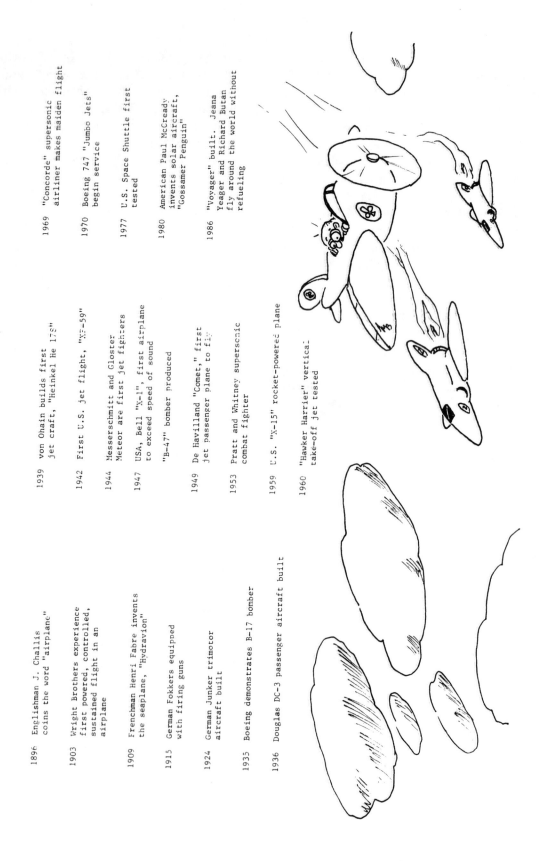

Fig. 2.15. An example of a time line.

Harpur, Patrick, Ed. *The Timetable of Technology*. New York: Hearst Books, 1982.

> The 20th century is chronicled in this large book with events from 1900 through 1982 outlined. In addition to the excellent visual chronology, stellar articles about inventions and technological developments in the last century and their resulting impact on life are included. Events in China, Russia, and England receive equal play to those which occurred in the United States.

McNeil, Mary Jean. *How Things Began*. London: Usborne Publishing, Ltd., 1979.

> This book is intended for children, but is an excellent beginning point for learners of all ages. The color illustrations may suggest ways for students to create their own time lines. Developments in the space race, motion pictures, bicycles, trains, balloons, castles, keeping clean, and telling time are featured. Although published in England, this and other Usborne books recommended here may be found in quality bookstores in the United States and Canada.

Reid, Struan. *Invention & Discovery*. London: Usborne Publishing Ltd., 1986.

> This, too, is a book intended for younger readers which may nonetheless prove useful as an entry point for students researching the chronology of inventions. Breakthroughs and landmark events in fields as diverse as solar energy, civil engineering, fertilizers and food, medicine, chemistry, painting, mathematics, and domestic appliances are chronicled.

A boxed kit containing several beautifully illustrated time lines is available from Educational In sights, Domineguez Hills, California 09220. A more expensive, but exceptionally complete time line is "The Illustrated Chart of History" which chronicles both ancient and modern history. It may be ordered from The Illustrated Chart of History, 131 30th Street, N.W., #6, Auburn, Washington 98002.

CLASSROOM EXPERTS

As stated in the introduction, gifted students should not be regimented to a point where they are learning the same material at the same rate. The introductory webbing activity (see figure 1.1, p. 5) no doubt alerted students to the wide array of topics of interest which can be researched and studied. There is far too much to know about the history of invention for any one student to master. One way to allow for the pursuit of individual interest yet not relinquish the need for classroom sharing is to have each student become the classroom expert on a given topic. The procedure is already in effect if each student is reading a biography about a different inventor. Take the idea further and assign each student the task of becoming the classroom expert on the evolution of a particular invention or series of inventions in a specific field. The subject can be the student's choice. In the classroom "brain trust" being created, learning is not limited to the knowledge the teacher, a single film, or one text can provide. The classroom is filled with experts, each one having an area of expertise different from that of his or her classmates.

Each student can prepare a standard fact sheet (see figure 2.16) which chronicles the history and development, current status, trivia, and contribution or importance of the invention for which he or she is responsible. The fact sheets can be duplicated for all other students for inclusion in an invention notebook, or they can be placed in a learning center where they are readily accessible to all students. The expert's task does not end with the preparation of a fact sheet, however. Whenever questions about computers, cameras, or contact lenses arise, the person who is the classroom expert in that area uses his or her expertise to answer the question or suggest possible avenues of research and resources for further inquiry. In this manner, the knowledge students possess is shared. No one person, teacher, or student dominates the class because of his or her role or brilliance. Rather, the concepts of cooperation and interdependence are reinforced. Moreover, a far greater level of expertise and a much greater knowledge base extends across the classroom than would be possible in any other way.

INVENTION FACT SHEET

INVENTION: Robot

BACKGROUND HISTORY OF INVENTOR:

No one person is responsible for robots. Interestingly, two writers of fiction more often receive recognition than inventors of real robots. Czech playwright Karl Capek coined the word robot in a 1921 play "R.U.R." (for "Rossum's Universal Robots"), and science fiction author Isaac Asimov created the "Three Laws of Robotics" in a 1941 story, "Reason." In 1954, George Devol received the first patent for the first programmable industrial robot. In 1956, Devol and Joseph Engelberger founded Unimation, Inc., the world's first robot company. In 1961, Unimation began to produce and market the first robot arms for the automobile industry.

SIGNIFICANT DATES AND RELATED HISTORY OF DEVELOPMENTS WHICH PRECEDED THE INVENTION:

The Greek poet Homer describes two golden female statues who assist Hephaestus. The Egyptians used animated statues in religious ceremonies. Animated figures and statues, especially related to clockmaking were produced in the Middle Ages and during the Renaissance. Leonardo da Vinci helped construct a mechanical lion in honor of Louis XII of France. Mechanized toys proliferated in the early 20th century. James Watt's steam governor was a necessary invention for automation and robotics to become possible.

IMPACT OF THE INVENTION:

Robots have helped significantly to revolutionize industrial production in many parts of the world. Robotics is a vital part of Japan's phenomenal economic growth, especially in the highly successful automobile industry. While robots may have the potential to displace human workers, they also can perform many tasks which are too hazardous for humans or which are repetitive and boring. Robots have been created to perform an amazing variety of tasks. In Australia, for example, a robot has been invented for shearing sheep. In Japan, robots have been created which serve the functions of guard dogs for the blind.

MOST RECENT DEVELOPMENTS AND/OR CHANGES IN THE INVENTION:

Current work with robots involves experimentation with and invention of sensors which approach or equal human sensing capabilities. Sensors will allow robots to interact with their environment in order to compensate for the unknown and unexpected. Artificial intelligence will allow robots to "think" and function largely on their own.

SUGGESTED RESOURCES FOR FURTHER INQUIRY:

Marsh, Peter. *Robots*. New York: Crescent Books, 1985.

Morris, Brian. *The World of Robots*. New York: Gallery Books, 1985.

Reichardt, Jasia. *Robots: Fact, Fiction, and Prediction*. New York: Penguin Books, 1978.

Fig. 2.16. An invention fact sheet for the invention "robot."

INVENTION GAMES

Gifted students are not immune to the joys found in learning through games. Sometimes educators have the mistaken notion that games are somehow wrong or inappropriate for gifted students, the presumption apparently being that they should only be exposed to the most boring possible pathways of learning information calculated to create the most dour of expressions. Gifted students love and thrive upon mental games. The burden for creating should not rest upon the shoulders of the instructor, either. Students have a chance to develop their creativity when they are provided with opportunities to create stimulating learning materials to share with others.

The following ideas are beginning suggestions for games which convey and test knowledge about inventors and inventions. Creative students will no doubt suggest many more inventive alternatives.

Figure 2.17 is an example of a game playing board designed to accompany a book on inventions.

MATCH INVENTIONS WITH NATIONS

Ask students to match famous inventions with their national origin. An example might include the following countries and inventions.

paper	Italy
automobile	Denmark
dynamite	China
tape recorder	France
piano	Germany
sewing machine	Sweden

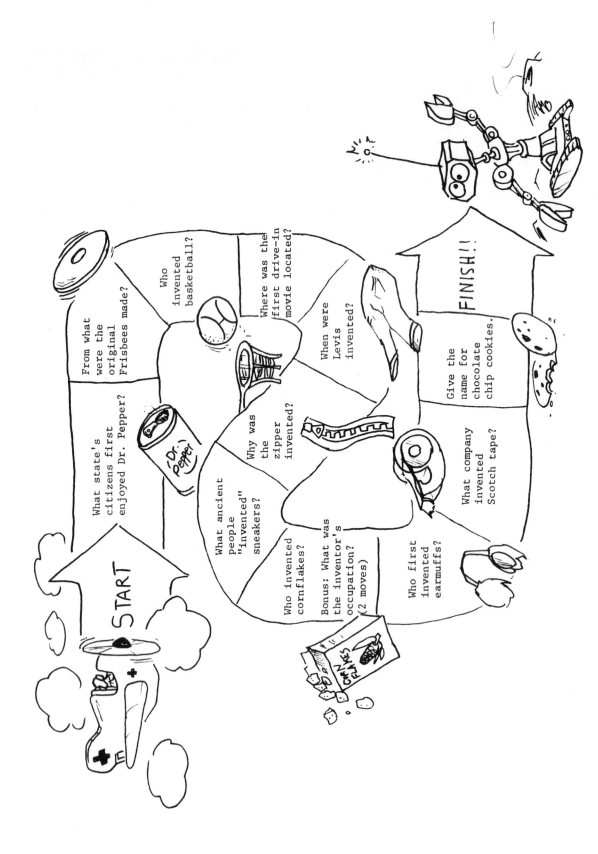

Fig. 2.17. A game board designed to accompany *Steven Caney's Invention Book* (New York: Workman Publishing Company, 1985).

CHRONOLOGIES

In conjunction with students' work with time lines, some may wish to create games based on the chronological order of inventions. For example, a game might involve placing the following inventions in the order in which each was invented

automobile	airplane	printing press	microscope
cotton gin	bicycle	television	transistor
telegraph	steam engine	radio	computer

WHO, WHAT, WHEN, WHERE

As students share information garnered from reading biographies, a game such as that shown in figure 2.18 may have appeal. The format is simple; basic information about inventors and their inventions is scrambled. The game player's task is to unscramble the information and correctly place the date, place, and invention with each inventor.

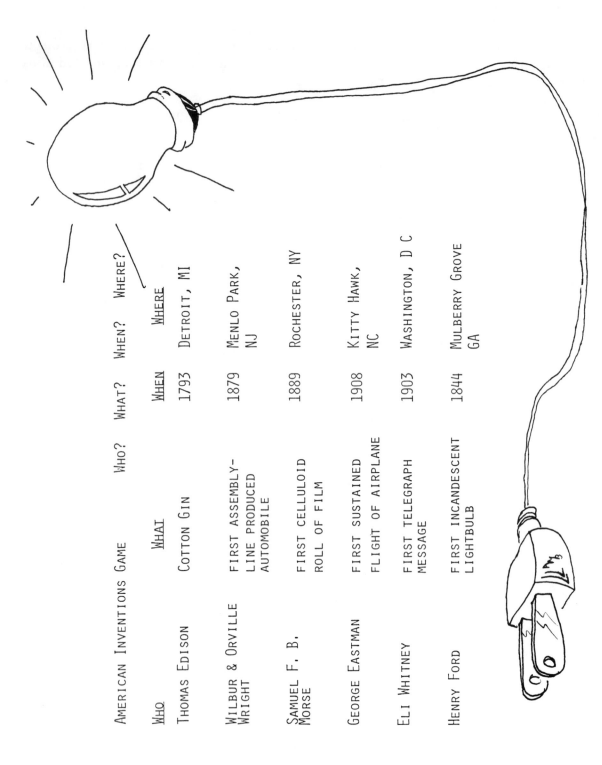

American Inventions Game			
Who?	What?	When?	Where?
Who	What	When	Where
Thomas Edison	Cotton Gin	1793	Detroit, MI
Wilbur & Orville Wright	First Assembly-Line Produced Automobile	1879	Menlo Park, NJ
Samuel F. B. Morse	First Celluloid Roll of Film	1889	Rochester, NY
George Eastman	First Sustained Flight of Airplane	1908	Kitty Hawk, NC
Eli Whitney	First Telegraph Message	1903	Washington, D C
Henry Ford	First Incandescent Lightbulb	1844	Mulberry Grove GA

Fig. 2.18. Who, What, When, Where game.

NOTES

[1]Michael H. Hart, *The 100: A Ranking of the Most Influential Persons in History* (New York: Galahad Books, 1978), 46.

[2]John Bartlett, *Familiar Quotations: A Collection of Passages, Phrases, and Proverbs Traced to Their Sources in Ancient and Modern Literature*, 15th ed., edited by Emily Morison Beck (Boston: Little, Brown and Company, 1980), 313.

[3]U.S. Department of Commerce, Patent and Trademark Office, *The Story of the U.S. Patent and Trademark Office* (Washington, D.C.: U.S. Government Printing Office, 1981).

[4]Christine Gorman, "A Mouse That Roared," *Time*, 25 April 1988, 83.

[5]Information supplied to the author from the Public Affairs Division of the U.S. Department of Commerce, Patent and Trademark Office.

[6]James Burke, *Connections* (Boston: Little, Brown and Company, 1978), 68.

[7]Ethlie Ann Vare and Greg Ptacek, *Mothers of Invention: From the Bra to the Bomb: Forgotten Women & Their Unforgettable Inventions* (New York: William Morrow and Company, Inc., 1988).

[8]Fred Amram, "The Innovative Woman," *New Scientist* 1411 (May 24, 1984): 10-12.

[9]*Ibid.*

[10]Joseph S. Renzulli, *The Enrichment Triad Model: A Guide for Developing Defensible Programs for the Gifted and Talented* (Wethersfield, Conn.: Creative Learning Press, 1977).

[11]The author wishes to thank officials at the Edison National Historic Site, of the National Park Service, U.S. Department of Interior for their assistance in providing the photo of page 1 of Edison's diary and photocopies of the diary text.

[12]Sidney J. Parnes, *The Magic of Your Mind* (Buffalo, N.Y.: Creative Education Foundation, Inc., 1978), 51.

3

Thoughts on Inventing, Invention, and Inventors

Millions of words have been spoken and written about inventing, invention, and inventors, as well as about individual inventions. Some express sentiments which now seem remarkably silly and shortsighted. The following quote has been attributed to both President William McKinley and a former director of the U.S. Patent Office, circa 1899, "Everything that can be invented has been invented." Regardless of who spoke these words at the turn of the century, he should have known better. Other invention-related quotations are much more profound and can serve teachers well in provoking the thinking of gifted students. Educators talk a great deal about thinking skills, but it is surprising how little time in school is devoted to reflection. One antidote is to ask students to digest, discuss, and debate the thoughts of others using quotations about inventions. The following quotes may be placed on overhead transparencies, on the chalkboard, or on individual cards placed in an invention learning center. Call attention to the quotes by asking students to write in their journals their reactions to a particular quote, or use a special quotation as a discussion starter about the meaning of invention. The reference section of the school LMC will most likely contain one or more books of quotations in which still more provocative statements about inventing, inventions, and inventors may be found.

QUOTATIONS

I invent nothing. I rediscover.
— Auguste Rodin

The principal mark of genius is not perfection but originality, the opening of new frontiers.
— Arthur Koestler

There is a correlation between the creative and the screwball. So we must suffer the screwball gladly.
— Kingman Brewster

Crank — a man with a new idea until it succeeds.
— Mark Twain

Imagination is more important than knowledge.
— Albert Einstein

The best way to have a good idea is to have lots of ideas.
— Linus Pauling

Necessity is the mother of invention.
— Latin Proverb

Invention is the mother of necessity.
— Thorstein Veblen

Invention breeds invention.
— Ralph Waldo Emerson

Invention is a combination of brains and material. The more brains you use, the less material you need.
— Charles F. Kettering

Ideas do not always have to be useful. Ideas can be inventions or they can solve problems or they can help people — or they can simply be fun. The mind is probably the least used source of enjoyment.
— Edward de Bono

Originality is simply a fresh pair of eyes.
— Woodrow Wilson

Genius is one percent inspiration and ninety-nine percent perspiration.

—Thomas Alva Edison

Minds are like parachutes. They only function when open.

—Anonymous

The only person who likes change is a wet baby!

—Roger von Oech

Our lives are often changed by the vision—and persistence—of individuals willing to pursue new ideas.

—P. Ranganath Nayak and John Ketteringham

If invention can be defined and codified, is it invention any longer?

—David N. Perkins

Anything one man can imagine, other men can make real.

—Jonathan Swift

Our heads are round so that our thinking can change direction.

—Francis Picabia

The reasonable person adapts himself to the world; the unreasonable one persists in trying to adapt the world to himself. Therefore, all progress depends upon the unreasonable man.

—George Bernard Shaw

Nothing is more important than to see the sources of invention, which are, in my opinion, more interesting than the inventions themselves.

—Gottfried Wilhelm Leibnitz

If it hadn't been for Edison, we'd be watching television by candlelight.

—Anonymous

Invention is the talent of youth, as judgment is of age.

—Jonathan Swift

Only an inventor knows how to borrow, and every man is or should be an inventor.

—Ralph Waldo Emerson

The march of invention has clothed mankind with powers of which a century ago the boldest imagination could not have dreamt.

—Henry George

A tool is but the extension of a man's hand, and a machine is but a complex tool. And he that invents a machine augments the power of a man and the well-being of mankind.

—Henry Ward Beecher

The universe is full of magical things patiently waiting for our wits to grow sharper.

—Eden Phillpotts

Great discoveries and improvements invariably involve the cooperation of many minds. I may be given credit for having blazed the trail but when I look at the subsequent developments I feel the credit is due to others rather than to myself.

—Alexander Graham Bell

We owe to the Middle Ages the two worst inventions of humanity—gunpowder and romantic love.

—André Maurois

High heels were invented by a woman who had been kissed on the forehead.

—Christopher Morley

Inventor: a person who makes an ingenious arrangement of wheels, levers and springs, and believes it civilization.

—Ambrose Bierce

Heaven

Hell is paved with good ~~intentions~~ inventions.

—Anonymous

The most powerful forces that change the way we live are the applied sparks of insight that we call invention.

—Dr. Robert Jarvik

4

The Present

One logical point of departure for an inquiry into invention as a phenomenon is to clarify the terminology often associated with invention and to examine the nature of invention. Both critical thinking and philosophy come into play in this pursuit.

WHAT IS INVENTION?

The first step is to define some terms. Place the following terms on the blackboard or on an overhead transparency:

invention	evolution
engineering	creativity
imagination	innovation
discovery	creation

Ask students to list the terms in their invention journals or notebooks and to first list their own definitions of the terms, followed by dictionary definitions. Conduct a class discussion centered on the definitions of the terms. If the class is going to be engaged in the study of inventing, inventions, and inventors for an extended period of time, it surely benefits all concerned to be on common ground with respect to the terminology. This is more than a vocabulary lesson; it is a lesson in semantics. It is especially important for the following discussion that all students share understandings of these terms. A possible initial discussion sequence is given in figure 4.1.

What is an invention? What is a discovery? How are they alike? Different? Is there a connecting link between the two things? An example for consideration: the invention of navigational instruments made further oceanic exploration possible. Increased interest in exploration spurred on the development of still newer navigational instruments.

What do you make of James Russell Lowell's thoughts, penned more than a century ago:

> If the works of the great poets teach anything, it is to hold mere invention somewhat cheap. It is not the finding of a thing, but the making something out of it after it is found, that is of consequence.

My Study Windows, 1871

Name a famous inventor. Name a famous discoverer. Were both names from the past? Can you name a contemporary inventor? (Dr. Robert Jarvik: artificial heart) Can you name a contemporary discoverer? (Jacques Cousteau; who is also an inventor—of the aqualung for diving)

What kinds of inventions are created? (There are inventions of new products, improvements on existing products, design inventions such as A. Bartholdi's Statue of Liberty, process inventions, plant variants, and now, even genetically engineered animals.) Are most inventions created to solve problems? Cite an example of an invention created to solve a problem. (The refrigerator prevents food spoilage.) Cite an example of an invention which solved a problem, but generated new problems which, in turn, demanded still newer inventions. (The invention of the automobile solved a transportation problem, namely getting from one place to another quickly and efficiently, but created pollution problems spurring the development of new carburetors.)

Fig. 4.1. Discussion of terms.

During this introductory exploration into the meaning of invention, it may be advantageous to discuss some of the more pithy statements on the subject found in the quotation section of this book. Any discussion of invention, its meaning, and its roots can profit from consideration of thoughts like those expressed by Rodin: "I invent nothing. I rediscover." and Einstein, "Imagination is more important than knowledge."

It is vital that gifted students flex their intellectual muscles and grapple with tough issues and questions without easy answers. It is entirely appropriate for these students to engage in discussions stimulated by provocative questions like these:

If invention can be defined, dissected, debated, and predicted, is it any longer invention?

Can one create something out of nothing? How can invention occur when something invented was not there before?

Do the times make the inventor or does the inventor make the times? To continue this probe, ask students to consider why the most famous inventors in American history were mostly contemporaries living in the latter part of the 19th century and the first part of the 20th century?

Is invention a form of evolution or vice versa?

The latter question can be explored further through these provocative questions: Are human beings the only inventors? Is mother nature perhaps the greatest inventor? Figure 4.2, a tool to use in this discussion, is an examination of the polar bear as inventor. Following a discussion of the polar bear's "invention" skills, some students may want to investigate the prowess of other animal inventors. For example, the beaver as an engineer and the gorilla as a tool user would both make interesting subjects for study.

Further discussions might be anchored around such topics as the origins of invention. Where do ideas come from? What mental processes is the inventor using during the act of invention? Do dreams play a role in creativity, discovery, and invention? Both Einstein and Tesla credited dreams as the source of at least some of their thinking.

THE POLAR BEAR AS INVENTOR

Few environments on the face of the Earth are more inhospitable than the Arctic, yet the polar bear finds it a delightful home due, it would seem, to his incredible inventiveness.

First, consider his coat. Note what scientists have to say about this ingenious invention:

> The shaggy fur of polar bears is 95% efficient in converting the sun's ultraviolet rays into usable heat. This remarkable "polar solar" phenomenon of converting sunlight into heat is unmatched by even the most expensive and sophisticated solar collectors, which have a maximum efficiency conversion of 65 to 70% (on a cold day, their efficiency is more like 20%). The unique property about the hairs in polar bear fur is that they are hollow and therefore act as a sort of tunnel. Light passes from the tip of each hair down to the bear's black skin, where it is converted into heat.[1]

The polar bear's hair functions in an analogous fashion to optical fibers used in telephone transmission lines. The polar bear's coat is not really white. The sun rays bouncing off the hair give it the white color which is a perfect camouflage for hunting in an all-white environment.

The polar bear also might be considered as the first inventor of the wet suit. Just below the layer of black skin, the polar bear has a thick coat of blubber which functions as a wet suit shielding the polar bear from the chilly Arctic waters.

The head and nose of the polar bear are longer than those found in other bears and suit the animal well for his environment. The longer nose gives the polar bear his incredibly keen sense of smell. (Scientists believe polar bears can smell a seal up to three miles distant.) Because of the acute sense of smell, this bear does not need to depend nearly so much upon hearing and therefore has quite small ears. Larger ears would likely stick out farther and freeze in the extremely cold environment. Even the small black nose may be a tricky invention. Some polar bear observers claim the polar bear is so smart he covers his nose with his paw as he approaches prey, allowing him 100 percent camouflage. Others claim that the polar bear is even shrewder. These observers claim that because of the ratio in size of the small black nose to the huge white body, the illusion is created in the vast arctic environment that the stalker is much farther away than he actually is. Seals and other prey may see the black nose of the polar bear, but make the fatal mistake of believing he is far off. Before they can react, the bear is upon them for the kill.

The polar bear depends upon at least one more invention which serves him well. His giant paws are one foot wide and eighteen inches long, with the striking force of a sledge-hammer. Moreover, the pads are rough like the bottom of a good boot to provide excellent traction on the treacherous ice. The claws are ideal for holding on to the slippery prey which make up the polar bear's diet.

Therefore, if one takes a broad view of invention, it surely can be argued that the polar bear is a remarkably clever inventor. For millions of years his inventions have served him well. Now, if he could only invent a way to confound his one enemy—man—he could live with near-perfect efficiency and economy.[2] (See polar bear illustration, p. 68.)

Fig. 4.2. A discussion in response to the question, "Are human beings the only inventors?"

WHAT ARE OUR MINDS DOING WHILE WE ARE INVENTING?

At this juncture, it may be time for a physical activity. One activity which sheds light on the preceding discussions is to have students take account of their thinking skills while engaged in the act of inventing.

Divide the class into aviation teams composed of four to six persons. Each group should choose a name for itself (e.g., The Fearless Falcon Flyers or The Red Baron Terrors) and appoint a recorder. Assign each group the task of designing and building a paper airplane which will soar as far as possible and stay aloft as long as possible. Establish whatever ground rules seem appropriate (e.g., no substance other than paper may be used in the construction.) Incidentally, there is no perfect set of rules. The author has used this exercise many times and has yet to find groups which did not find ways to legally circumvent his instructions. Of course, the competing groups yell "Foul!" This should not be seen as a problem, however. The great inventors have always broken established rules and have done what was said to be impossible.

Instruct the teams, especially recorders, to pay particular attention to all mental processes used by the group as they proceed through the task. What mental activity goes into the invention act? It may be necessary to suggest in advance some processes which students are likely to encounter and rely upon: memory, observation, imitation, trial and error, discovery, evaluation, intuition, and analysis. It may not be appropriate to evaluate or judge the student descriptors originally, but it would make an excellent follow-up activity. For example, is trial and error a mental process? If not, what mental processes are involved in trial and error procedures? Students can list, defend, and debate the various terms used in the activity.

It may be additionally useful to ask each team to appoint a second person to record all the positive and negative statements made during the inventing process. Then, another aspect of the debriefing process can be an examination of the roles played by criticism and encouragement in the inventing process.

After a reasonable length of time, ask each group to launch its aircraft. Prizes may be awarded for the criteria already mentioned, time and distance, as well as for the design of the craft itself and the launch team performance.

Debrief by thoroughly discussing all the intelligences or mental processes used in the act of invention. If gifted students do operate at a differentiated and sophisticated level of cognitive functioning, it seems imperative that they have some idea of what is happening when they use thinking skills.

Some students may want to turn to further investigations of thinking skills and brain functions. The whole field of hemispheric brain functioning will be fascinating and appealing for some gifted students. Indeed, some of these students may ultimately become the cognitive psychologists and neurophysiologists who unlock the mysteries of the brain. They may note that many of our greatest contemporary and past inventors are thought to be or to have been "right brain" dominant thinkers.

Regardless of the extent to which students generate further studies from this initial activity, all should understand that invention results from complex cognitive processing.

One fine resource which examines how contemporary inventors think and work is *Inventors at Work: Interviews with 16 Notable American Inventors* by Kenneth A. Brown (Redmond, Washington: Tempus Books, 1988). The inventors with whom Brown speaks include Paul MacCready, inventor of the Gossamer Condor, Wilson Greatbatch, inventor of the implantable pacemaker, Harold Rosen, inventor of the first geosynchronous satellite which allowed for instantaneous worldwide communication, and Nat Wyeth (brother to famed artist Andrew Wyeth), who created the modern plastic soda bottle. Each of the 16 inventors talks about how he or she works, makes unique connections, and arrives at the stage of creating something new to the world.

HOW DOES IT WORK?

While it is not a prerequisite to possess a Ph.D. in physics to be an inventor, certainly a little knowledge of how things work is essential. An inventions unit is a beautiful opportunity to make science a vital part of the curriculum. The teacher should not be alarmed if he or she does not have an extensive background. Now is the time to call on community mentors, parents of the students who are engineers, physicists, and chemists, the school system's science curriculum director, a retired high school physics or industrial arts teacher, the current building science and industrial arts teachers, *and* the classroom experts who are the mechanically and spatially gifted students in class. These are the students who know how things work. Recognize, however, that some of these students may not be good test-takers and may not automatically be found in programs for gifted students identified in traditional ways.

If the other students are going to be inventors, they also need to have at least a rudimentary knowledge of tools and machines. The age and sophistication of the students will determine how basic the first lessons need to be. It is essential to first diagnose the sophistication of science knowledge and skills students already possess. Students should be familiar with the six simple machines: the lever, inclined plane, pulley, screw, wedge, and wheel and axle. Apropos to the latter, students should understand gear ratios and how they are computed. Additionally, students should have a basic understanding of the more basic laws of physics, gravity and energy, and electricity, magnetism, and electromagnetism.

Students should also gain an appreciation for the workings of some of the appliances and machines which are vital to their daily lives, but the precise workings of which are quite probably unknown and taken for granted. Assign each student one invention about which he or she will learn its workings or operation. The following is but a small sampling of possible choices:

VCR	toaster	fluorescent light
bicycle	telephone	television
vending machine	automobile engine	video game
tape recorder	watch or clock	electric motor
batteries	camera	computer
microwave oven	artificial satellite	

It is the task of each student to determine how the invention he or she is assigned operates. Remind students to keep all research notes in their invention notebooks or journals. A variety of procedures can be utilized for the presentation of material. Demonstrations and presentations need not be excessively long, and one can be scheduled each day as the beginning class activity. If students choose to present their information via brief written fact sheets or as part of an interest center, no class time need be assigned or budgeted. It is wise to allow students plenty of latitude in determining a presentation format. Part of the learning experience is the creativity used and developed in determining *how* to share *what* they have learned. Do not be alarmed if a sagacious student invites a nuclear physicist to class to explain the workings of nuclear power plants. Just recall Newton's Third Law of Motion: for every action there is an opposite and equal reaction. This student is quite probably exerting as much energy and using as many communications skills in enlisting the expert's cooperation and arranging for the expert's visitation and presentation as if he or she worked solo.

While students may be guided to the numerous print resources which explain how things work, also allow them a variety of options for finding resources. Do not lock students into using only one kind of resource and, in doing so, inadvertently prohibit them from enjoying some side benefits to their research. Example: Susan can learn how a clock works by reading a book. However, she can also meet and come to know Mr. Shugg, who lives just down the street, and who has spent his entire adult life as a watch maker and repairman. He can become an excellent mentor for Susan and pass on to her at least a piece of his vast knowledge. Similarly, Tom can learn a little bit about what his older sister does in her work in the Air Force as a satellite tracker while she explains to him the workings of artificial satellites.

A few of the many excellent print resources worthy of note are listed below. The reference and science sections of most public libraries contain quite adequate materials to answer most questions students will have.

How Things Work. Washington, D.C.; National Geographic Society, 1983.

Leokum, Arkady. *Tell Me Why: Answers to Hundreds of Questions Children Ask.* New York: Grosset & Dunlap, 1986.

Macaulay, David. *The Way Things Work.* Boston: Houghton Mifflin Company, 1988.

The Way Things Work. New York: Simon and Schuster, 1967.

AN INVENTION EXERCISE

Divide the class into teams of four or five students. Explain to students that the Smithsonian Institution Traveling Exhibition Service is planning a traveling exhibit of some of Edison's products. Part of the exhibit will feature the last remaining, original, working light bulbs created by Edison. A lucrative contract will be awarded to the company which invents a packaging system to protect these valuable artifacts while they are in transit.

Bring to class four or five old light bulbs which are discolored. Demonstrate that each light bulb still works by screwing it into a lamp, plugging the lamp into an electrical outlet, and turning the light switch on. Give each team one of the light bulbs with instructions that they are one of the competing packaging companies and that their task is to package the bulb in such a way that it will not break or cease to work even when the package itself is roughly treated. Explain that this is a test, and that the company which best succeeds the test will win the contract. Each team must also submit a cost analysis of the expense of packaging. In the event of a tie among competitors, the final contract will go to the company which submits the lowest bid.

Choose a safe height of at least one story from which the packages may be dropped by a member of the team or by the teacher. Note that it is crucial to establish safety procedures so no student is endangered in the release of the package. After all the packages are dropped, they are carried back to the classroom, carefully opened, and observations are made to determine which light bulbs remain unbroken, and which, if any, still work. The team which has the lowest bid *and* a working light bulb wins the Smithsonian contract.

Teams will enjoy seeing the multiplicity of ways and means which inventive people can use to solve a common problem.

A RUBRIC FOR INVENTING

B. Edward Shlesinger, Jr. is a patent attorney who holds over 100 U.S. patents. He is also an indefatigable promoter of invention activities for students through his writings and his work with teachers, students, and schools. His source book for inventing in the classroom, *How to Invent*, is probably the definitive book on the process of inventing for school use. It is certainly a must for teachers planning to introduce students to the art of invention.

Shlesinger's number one theme is that invention is not a mysterious and enigmatic art form practiced only by an elite group of geniuses.

> Invention is nothing more than correlating the information which we have at our fingertips to make something that has not been made before. Six-year-olds have millions of bits of information stored in their computer-like brains. Show them how to correlate information and they readily become inventors. Six-year-olds recognize the concepts of "comb" and "triangle." When they are instructed to put these two concepts together, they invent new triangular combs. Eli Whitney put together the concepts of "comb" and "cylinder" in 1793 and invented the cotton gin.[3]

In his text and many articles, Shlesinger specifies a rubric of *five* essential invention steps to teach students:

identification

foundation

data

imagination

limitation

First, teach students to look for problems. What is a source of annoyance or inconvenience for people which might be ameliorated with a new invention. Though Shlesinger does not cite the following example, it seems an apt one. The heat build-up in locked, parked cars was an annoyance to people on sunny, hot days for many years, yet only recently did an inventor think to solve the problem quite simply with the invention of the now ubiquitous folding auto windshield sun screens. It is an example of problem finding leading to invention. Teach students not just to be problem solvers, but problem finders as well.

Once a problem area has been identified and students are hot on the invention trail, Shlesinger suggests they need to lay the *foundation* for all their further work. They should acquire fundamental background information about the kind of invention they propose. For example, if a student decides to invent a new kind of toy, then it behooves him to investigate related developments in the history of toy invention. Shlesinger also suggests students become familiar with established classification systems respective to their proposed invention. One excellent source he cites is the *Manual of Classification of Patents* published by the U.S. Patent Office and available from the U.S. Government Printing Office. In addition to learning something about the history of the proposed toy invention, it may serve the prospective inventor well to know that there are over 200 classes into which toy inventions fall. An awareness of such classification systems may open up new avenues of thinking about their inventions which students had not previously considered. One of the most uttered cliches is "Why reinvent the wheel?" It has merit here. Teach students to inquire into what already exists and how it came to be before they go forth to create the new.

Data is an essential possession for prospective inventors. Once the path of problem solving and inventing has been chosen, the students need to learn all they can about their proposed inventions. The classic five W questions (who, what, when, where, why plus how) are the tools to be used in this inquiry. Who will use the proposed invention? How will it be used? When? Where? How will it be made? When and where can it be produced?

When sufficient data has been gathered and analyzed, all systems are go. It is time for *imagination* to take over. At this point, the student looks for new combinations of existing concepts, is alert to new ways of perceiving the world, and always keeps an open mind. Trial and error, combinations, substitutions, and rearrangements may be tried. The invention is metamorphisizing, being born during this stage.

The final stage in Shlesinger's rubric is the consideration of *limitations*. Build a better mousetrap and the world will beat a path to one's door. Right? Wrong. The mousetrap may be so expensive to produce that no one will spend the money to buy one. The market for mousetraps may be so saturated that no one will buy the invention no matter how good it is. Or, the competition may be so fierce in the mousetrap industry that the inventor of the latest and greatest one will have to devote most of his or her energy justifying and protecting the invention. Isaac Asimov shares a classic invention story which illustrates this latter point. In the battle of the currents, Edison unscrupulously lobbied for Tesla's alternating current to be used as the source for New York State's new electric chair, and then publicly pointed to this example of the terrible, deadly nature of alternating current.[4] The point is students need to consider the feasibility of manufacturing and marketing their inventions. Will the end result be worth the time and expense expended?

As with the processes of critical and creative thinking and problem solving, there are many competing models which teachers and students can use. Shlesinger's model is not the only approach, but it does appear to be a very good one. And, it has the added credibility of being proposed by an inventor who has used the model himself in his production of more than 100 patented inventions.[5]

CONNECTING WITH CPS, SCAMPER, SYNECTICS, AND OTHER FAVORITE TOOLS UTILIZED IN CURRICULA FOR THE GIFTED AND TALENTED

Many of the models and tools which have been widely utilized for more than a decade by educators of gifted and talented students are quite applicable and transferable to curriculum focused upon inventing. Indeed, there is a striking resemblance between Shlesinger's invention process rubric and the creative problem-solving model. Processes such as synectics, attribute listing, morphological analysis, and SCAMPER not only complement and interface with Shlesinger's five-point plan for inventing, they take on new meaning and purpose when linked to the art of invention. As the author noted in the introduction, there is too much of a tendency in educational programs for the gifted and talented to emphasize process skills and tools (e.g., rote learning of the classes and verbs found in Bloom's taxonomy) while failing to help students make meaningful connections of these processes with content and product, or to generalize the use of the processes to real and significant problems. Merely introducing students to attribute listing as a problem-solving tool and using it in an abstract classroom exercise of redesigning a shopping mall is suspect. Students need immediate and real opportunities to employ this tool if it is to be internalized, valued, and have any real potential for ultimate transfer and general usage. Teaching attribute listing in conjunction with the foundation and data stages of the invention process, for example, allows students to immediately apply, utilize, and note the value of the tool, and greatly enhances its chances of becoming a vital and often used part of their cognitive functioning.

In the following pages, each of several process models and tools widely used in programs for the gifted and talented will be explained *and* related to the invention process.

CREATIVE PROBLEM SOLVING (CPS)

Creative Problem Solving (CPS) is analogous to the invention process in that there are numerous process models. The most widely used and copied model is the Creative Problem-Solving Institute's five-stage model outlined by Ruth B. Noller, Sydney J. Parnes, and Angelo M. Biondi of the Creative Education Foundation.[6] It is the model utilized by the National Future Problem Solving Program which serves as an adjunct to many programs for gifted and talented students in the United States and Canada. The five steps or stages are:

fact-finding

problem-finding

idea-finding

solution-finding

acceptance-finding

In the first stage, *fact-finding*, the potential problem solver analyzes the problematic situation which he or she confronts. The problem solver is critically aware of the importance of remaining open-minded, and uses divergent thinking to consider all possible causes of the current problem. He or she collects all the data he or she can which will aid in determining the real underlying problem. The problem solver then analyzes the "mess" carefully and thoroughly, taking special care not to be too hasty in defining the problem incorrectly due to the lack of adequate data or through failure to consider all aspects or facets of a problematic situation. As in the data-gathering segment of the invention process, the news reporter's five Ws suffice as handy tools.

Once the problem solver believes he or she has a solid understanding of all the dynamics associated with the problem, he or she engages in *problem-finding* which chiefly relies upon convergent thinking. From the multitude of possible problem statements, the problem solver asks the question: What is the *key* problem? It has been suggested that the uncreative mind can spot wrong answers, but it takes a creative mind to spot wrong questions. One educational film, *Creative Problem Solving: How to Get Better Ideas*, illustrates the vital role the *problem-finding* stage plays in the overall process of creative problem solving. The film recounts a real-life problem situation in which invention played an important role. In the scenario, produce farmers were confronted with an unacceptably high level of crop damage and loss when mechanical harvesters picked tomatoes in the field. Tinkering with the harvesters yielded no successful gains on the problem. Finally, it occurred to the researchers that they had not defined the original problem correctly. They had focused all their attention and resources upon the problem of building a better machine. When they redefined the problem and shifted the focus to the tomato rather than the machine, they were rather quickly able to solve the problem. Horticulturists created a new hybrid tomato which was both more accessible to the harvester and less susceptible to machine damage. As the film's narrator points out, a better problem-solving approach may be to ask not how to build a better mousetrap, but how to get rid of mice.[7]

Students nearly always want to rush this stage of the CPS model. The tomato harvesting example and countless others drawn from the real world are proof that the problem-finding and defining stage should be passed through very cautiously and judiciously. The problem statement is the basis for all energies and expenses expended throughout the rest of the problem-solving process. The person or corporation who spends thousands or even millions of dollars and untold hours attempting to solve the wrong problem is going to be frustrated, and perhaps, bankrupt. Time wisely invested at the front end of the problem solving process ultimately pays off in the end results.

Typically, problem statements begin with one of the two stem phrases:

How might I/we.....?

In what ways might I/we?

This phase of the CPS model appears to interface well with, and perhaps even enhance, the identification phase of Shlesinger's inventing rubric. In identifying problems to be solved with their inventions, students need to allow adequate time for research and deliberation to consider many aspects of any problematic situation and to be confident they are attacking the right problem. Another example of real-life application of this dictum which may be worth sharing with students can be found in *Guided Design* by Charles E. Wales and Robert Stager:

> Identifying the problem and stating the goal are extremely important steps in the solution of any problem. An example of this (importance) occurred in the early stages of the U.S. space program when a similar problem to the following was posed.

> Find a material which will withstand a temperature of 14,000 F for five minutes.

> Of course this problem was related to re-entry of a space capsule and the enormous amount of heat generated during the process. A great deal of money and time was wasted trying to solve this problem because there was no known material which would withstand the required temperature. Finally, someone realized that they were trying to solve the wrong problem. The new problem was stated as follows:

> Find a way to protect a capsule and the person inside during re-entry.

> The problem was solved very quickly with the ablation system now in use.[8]

The third stage of the CPS model is *idea-finding*. This stage of the model is very much the counterpart of the *imagination* phase of inventing. The thinking mode shifts from convergent to divergent with a vengence. Here the problem solver considers all possible ways and manners of solving the stated problem. Ridiculous ideas are never discounted. The mind is allowed to wander. If ideas cease to flow, this is an excellent point to employ ancillary creative thinking tools like SCAMPER (see the following discussion). The more ideas the problem solver generates, the more options he or she has and the more likely he or she will be able to find a really effective solution to the stated problem. Likewise, the more options the inventor considers during the imagination phase, the greater the likelihood the resulting invention will effectively overcome the original problem identified.

Once a problem solver has a long list of viable options, he or she is ready to become once again more convergent and evaluative in his or her thinking in order to make clear and wise choices from among the many options generated. But how are such decisions made? In the *solution-finding* phase of the problem-solving process, the problem solver first identifies appropriate criteria and then uses the criteria to make judgments about the many ideas generated. Typically, the problem solver wants to consider the advantages and disadvantages of his or her many proposed solutions from the vantage point of several different criteria. Certainly, he or she may want to consider the criterion of cost. Any given idea may first appear to be a wonderful solution to a problem, but in the cold, hard light of dollars and cents, reality demands reconsideration. In more recent times, thankfully, both government and business agencies have had to consider environmental impact as an important criterion in any decision-making exercise. The following list is a sampling of some of the many criteria which may be used to evaluate proposed solutions:

Which proposed solution will be easiest to implement?

Which proposed solution will be the most economical to implement?

Which proposed solution will be the most popular with the personnel or constituency directly involved?

Which proposed solution is the most ethical?

Which proposed solution will be the most rapidly implemented?

Which proposed solution will be the most likely to work?

Obviously, the specific problem identified will dictate which criteria are chosen as the yardstick of evaluation in a given situation. There is no absolute right number of criteria to choose, but it would be a rare instance where only one criterion would work. The problem solver may initially say he or she is only interested in the answer to the question: Which proposed solution will work best? But, what happens when he or she later learns that the cost of producing or realizing the solution is greater than any benefit yielded? Three to five criteria usually can be generated which will give the problem solver an effective and manageable assessment. Considerable thought should go into the selection of appropriate criteria. On more than one occasion the author has had students go all the way through the evaluation procedure only to discover that their final, proposed solution is unworkable. Usually, the students have selected a solution which fared well under the scrutiny of the criteria of ease, economy, and quickness of implementation, but they neglected to include as a criterion: Will it work?

Once the problem solver has identified his or her criteria for evaluation, it is time to pare down the list of many options to a manageable number for the final review and evaluation. It is typically rather easy, especially with the chosen criteria fresh in mind, to narrow the list down to 10 finalists. To make the final selection process both graphic and easier to complete, a grid is suggested (see figure 4.3).[9] Here the criteria are listed across the horizontal axis of a grid, while the best proposed solutions are listed vertically. The problem solver uses one criterion at a time as a yardstick and evaluates all the proposed solutions by that criterion. Once again, there is no absolute as to the scoring system utilized. The problem solver may use pluses and minuses, for example. However, the author has found that a forced ranking of the proposed solutions is more discriminating and ultimately yields a more definitive choice or answer when the exercise is finished. Hence, figure 4.3 shows the use of a forced ranking among the options using a scale of 1 to 10 points, where a 10 represents the proposed solution which *best* meets each of the respective criterion. In the sample grid, additional spaces are provided to indicate which ideas will be used, which will be rejected outright, which might be used at some later time, and which ideas might be used if they could be modified in some positive way to overcome current liabilities.

In this example of *solution-finding*, students are exploring options for the future of ocean farming in an activity sponsored by the National Future Problem-Solving Program. The problem identified by students is:

How might the United States help an economically underdeveloped coastal nation achieve greater economic independence and stability through the establishment of an undersea farming program?

Criteria chosen for the solution-finding stage of the CPS process are:

Which solution would be the most acceptable to all parties?
Which solution would have the most long-lasting benefits for the people of the coastal nation?
Which solution would cost the least to implement?
Which solution would have the greatest potential for producing ancillary or spin-off benefits?
Which solution would be the most environmentally sound?

From the nearly 30 ideas generated during the *idea-finding* stage of creative problem solving, the students selected 10 ideas for final evaluation.

1. Form Peace Corps units specifically trained in aquaculture.

2. Encourage Russia and other United Nations countries to make the effort a joint venture and model project for all developing coastal nations.

3. Provide tax incentives to private U.S. businesses which will lend ocean farming equipment and technical assistance to the coastal nation.

4. Establish a model of the U.S. Department of Agriculture Extension Service in the coastal country which will make use of satellite communication.

5. Provide government grants to universities which will lend faculty assistance to the coastal nation in a five-year development period.

6. Sponsor an international lottery game to generate revenue for the development phases of the aquaculture project.

7. Provide military service credit to individuals willing to spend two years of service in the coastal nation as part of teams developing the aquaculture project.

8. Develop an advertising campaign featuring famous U.S. citizens selling the aquaculture project both in the United States and in the coastal nation.

9. Secure the cooperation and participation of U.S. service groups such as the Kiwanis and Boy Scouts to make the aquaculture project a major volunteer project.

10. Secure the approval and cooperation for the aquaculture project from all political factions and groups within the coastal nation.

(Fig. 4.3 continues on page 78.)

Fig. 4.3—*Continued*

SOLUTION-FINDING GRID

IDEA-FINDING CHOICES	ACCEPTABILITY	LASTING BENEFITS	COSTS	POTENTIAL	ENVIRONMENT	TOTAL SCORE	USE	REJECT	HOLD FOR FUTURE USE	POSSIBLE MODIFICATIONS
	CRITERIA							OTHER OPTIONS		
Peace Corps Units	10	9	1	7	7	34	√			
Russia/U.N. Participation	4	6	8	9	10	37			√	
Tax Incentives	3	3	5	2	3	16		√		
Extension Services	6	10	4	8	8	36	√			
University Grants	5	2	3	6	6	22			√	Consider combining with ext. service
Lottery Game	1	4	7	1	2	15		√		
Military Service Credit	8	5	6	5	5	29			√	Combine with Peace corps
Advertising Campaign	7	1	2	4	1	15		√		
Service Clubs	9	7	9	3	4	32			√	add as phase 2 of plan
Coastal Nation Cooperation	2	8	10	10	9	39	√			

Proposed Solution: Combine several alternatives into one overall plan. Education and service would be at the center of the plan of attack.

Fig. 4.3. Solution finding.

The *solution-finding* phase of the CPS model combined with the final stage, *acceptance-finding*, represent the activity Shlesinger proposes as the *limitation* phase of his model for inventors. In *acceptance-finding*, the problem solver is concerned with implementing the chosen solution for solving the designated problem. Once again, the five W questions come in to play. Who will implement the solution? When, where, and how will it be implemented? In this final phase of the CPS model, the problem solver comes up with a plan of action.

Perhaps the most critical and chronic problem related to the use of the CPS model in programs for the gifted and talented is the neglect of the essential *acceptance-finding* phase. Far too often the "fun" parts of the CPS model receive attention, but the hard and practical work of implementing creative ideas is slighted. Often this occurs because the problematic situations students are given to solve are abstract and beyond their reasonable ability or resources to impact. Students need realistic and complete problem-solving experiences to help them realize that the most difficult and time-consuming aspect of problem solving is often the implementation stage. It does not take a great deal of personal effort or commitment to generate a lot of bright, creative ideas. But, some individual or group usually has to work hard and long to translate bright ideas into action steps. This is why the CPS model applied to inventing can be so vital. Students need real problems with which to grapple if they are to ultimately become expert problem solvers. With inventing as the focus, students can identify manageable problems, consider viable alternatives, select the best and most workable ideas from among the alternatives, and proceed to physically invent and implement their solution.[10]

A particularly valuable invention resource to consult for real-life examples of the *acceptance-finding* stage of the CPS model operationalized is *Breakthroughs* by Ranganath Nayak and John M. Ketteringham. The authors have this to say about the necessity of combining ingenuity with other factors:

> Ingenuity is a step, not an end in itself. Inventors, more accurately, have greater power than anyone else to trigger breakthroughs, but once invented, a concept must be manufacturable, marketable, and competitive. Inventors need help. So do clever marketers. Eventually, to be commercially successful, a concept requires a measure of organizational cohesion — *teamwork*.[11]

Nayak and Ketteringham share a variety of stories about how products people now take for granted made it to the marketplace. Included in this excellent book are the stories behind VCRs, microwave ovens, the Walkman, and Nautilus equipment.

SCAMPER

Bob Eberle was inventive in rearranging many of the creativity techniques spelled out by Alex Osborne into a handy acronym which is taught and employed in programs for gifted and talented students.[12] Explicated, SCAMPER means:

Substitute

Combine

Adapt/Adjust

Modify, Minify, Magnify

Put to other uses

Eliminate, Elaborate

Reverse, Rearrange

Once it is learned by students, the acronym serves as a useful mnemonic device to draw upon both in the *idea-finding* stage of the CPS model and in the *imagination* phase of inventing. Recall Shlesinger's statement that invention may be viewed as the combination of known concepts to create new things.

One young man's invention exhibited at a recent invention fair for junior high school students demonstrated the power of the SCAMPER effect. The youth invented an umbrella for portable mixers, *combining* the concepts mixer and umbrella. A small, doll-size plastic umbrella can be easily attached and detached from the handle of the mixer. The bottom circumference of the umbrella when extended open is approximately equal to the circumference of a large mixing bowl. Voila! No more spattering of chocolate cake batter all over the kitchen cabinets, counters, and floors. When the mixing is done, a quick cleaning of the umbrella with a damp sponge takes care of all errant cake batter.

The bicycle industry has been rejuvenated by *adapting* the standard bicycle to perform in rough terrain. Millions of dirt bikes are now sold each year. Enterprising inventors and entrepreneurs have seized the concept of *minification* with the introduction of light foods, beer, etc. A ski resort in the Pacific Northwest, where it is often very damp, has found *new uses* for plastic garbage bags. Whistler Ski Resort prints their trademark/logo on garbage bags precut to provide openings for the head and arms of skiers. On wet, drizzly days the new ski apparel sells like the proverbial hotcakes to the intrepid skiers.

Anyone engaged in creative thinking, problem solving, and inventing can profit from a jump start to get the brain fully functioning. In their creation of inventions, students should be habitually asking themselves how they can use the SCAMPER processes to improve existing products and to make their newest inventions even better.

ATTRIBUTE LISTING

Another excellent tool used to provoke minds into considering new possibilities is *attribute listing*. The format is simple. The inventor or problem solver simply takes the object, institution, or whatever is the primary focus of concern and breaks it down into its basic, characteristic component parts. Then he or she considers all the possible values of each of the attributes. For example, the problem solver or inventor may determine that some new configuration of the school desk is needed. He or she first considers the common attributes of school desks. The final list of attributes include these things:

the *frame material* is wood

The *seat* is also made of wood and is of a fixed height

it has a *writing surface* which is wood covered with formica

Now, the student considers the possible values of the attribute "frame." He or she lists various materials including metal and plastic which would make suitable, if not overly comfortable, frames. Then, the problem solver thinks of how scratched and dirty desks become after years of use and often, abuse, and wonders why desks could not be made from paper. If desks could be molded from very heavy, compacted paper, perhaps they could then be recycled at the end of each school year, reformed, and schools would have fresh new desks for students each year. Moving on through the list of attributes, the student plays around with possible values of the seat attribute. He or she recalls the complaints of fellow students about how hard and uncomfortable the school's wooden desk seats are. When the new paper desks are first being made and later formed and remolded after recycling, perhaps it might be possible to mold in foam rubber seats. Then it occurs to the inventor to change the shape of the seat. If the new desks are being molded, perhaps they can be created with contoured seats to better fit the human form. Lastly, he or she thinks about the writing surface. The function of the school desks really has not changed in a long time, and they are not much different in form and function than those his parents, or even grandparents, used. Yet the needs of students have changed dramatically. Today, a student may need a computer and almost certainly a calculator. Could the desk be redesigned to have the writing surface become a combination keyboard, calculator, and monitor? Once again the inventor or problem solver is considering whole new avenues and options because he or she has taken time to examine something as seemingly simply made as a school desk. The problem solver has examined its component parts or attributes, and has posited new values for each of the attributes.

Attribute listing can assist students in several phases of the CPS and invention processes. Certainly, it may be used with *fact-finding* and *problem-finding*. Sometimes what at first appears to be a major problem is, in fact, merely the dysfunctioning of one small attribute of a product or system. Isolating and examining the attributes will yield this insight on the problem. This tool may also be useful in both the *foundation* and *data* phases of the invention process. Students may better classify, research, and learn detailed information about a proposed invention by attending to its component parts.

MORPHOLOGICAL FORCED CONNECTIONS

This tool takes *attribute listing* a step further. Once all the possible values of each attribute are listed, new products are suggested when new, random connections are made among all the attributes. Don Koberg and Jim Bagnall illustrate the use of the procedure in excellent fashion in *The All-New Universal Traveler*. After designating the attributes of a ball-point pen as being shape, substance, cap, and cartridge, the authors generate several possible values for each attribute. Randomly working across the stated attributes, they propose a new invention: a pen in the shape of a cube, which has no cover, writes on one corner, and has six faces for advertising, photographs, and calendars.[13] Here again is a tool which does not promise to yield brilliant results every time it is used, but which does serve as a catalyst to keep the mind of the inventor or problem solver flexible and open to myriad possibilities.

FORCED RELATIONSHIPS

Sometimes ideas really do appear to come out of nowhere and when least expected. *Forced relationships* plays upon this notion of serendipity. When people are engaged in inventing or problem solving, a facilitator can provoke a whole new line of thinking and discovery by asking the deliberators to consider words or objects which he or she provides, usually randomly, and to forge a new invention or solution which includes the given words or objects. In other words, a new relationship between what exists and the new stimuli is forced. The facilitator or teacher might require a student puzzling over new school desk designs to figure the concepts "forest" and "weather" into his or her creative thinking equation. Each individual or group will, of course, come up with different reactions. Perhaps a young man working on the desk design example will decide to have each desk surface monitor equipped with a small strip at the top or bottom of the screen which, when activated by the desk computer, will provide time, weather, and temperature. He may also be prompted by the "forest" cue to decide that school is often overly stressful for students and that they need time to relax and reflect. Therefore, he decides to build into the desk an imagery program. The desk has a jack and is equipped with a pair of earphones. At the student's cue to the computer, tranquil and peaceful forest sounds are played. After a five-minute interval, the tape gently reminds the student to return to his or her studies.

One invention story, perhaps apocryphal, is that the General Electric Company developed the photographic flash cube after a team of product development engineers working on flash bulb alternatives were prompted with the two words "fire" and "ice." The author finds *forced relationships* to be an especially interesting tool in stimulating students to think more creatively.

It often yields only bizarre or seemingly silly suggestions. But, about one time in ten, it appears to be just the catalyst students need to break through a mental log jam and to develop strikingly original and fresh approaches to problem solving.

SYNECTICS

Synectics involves complicated and sophisticated processes and more correctly may be considered as a model on the order of Shlesinger's process of invention or the CPS model than as a tool occasionally employed to stimulate creative thinking.

Since 1945, W. J. J. Gordon has sought ways to help ordinary people systematically develop the types of creative insights and breakthroughs which are legend in the lives and works of creative geniuses. He indeed believes that a *method* can be learned which will bring about, quite deliberately, creative insights. In other words, genius, or at least high levels of creative functioning, need not be left to chance.

In a paper entitled "Toward Understanding 'The Moment of Inspiration,' " Gordon and coauthor Tony Poze list four abstract psychological states necessary for creative connections to occur: *detachment, involvement, deferment,* and *speculation.*[14] They state further that these psychological states do not occur just because we will them. However, their likelihood of occurrence is greatly improved when metaphorical thinking is promoted. The heart of Synectics, as promulgated by Gordon and Poze, lies in the three metaphorical tools suggested: *direct analogy, personal analogy*, and *compressed conflict*. The working model and strategies of Synectics are far more complex, sophisticated, and involved than a brief discussion here can do justice. A brief description of each of the three metaphorical tools is given here and a connection to the act of invention is made and explored as regards the particularly relevant tool of *direct analogy*.

In the use of the *personal analogy*, the problem solver strives for empathy through presumed identity with the object, question, or issue at hand. The student attempting to invent a new spoon might ask him or herself, "How would I feel if I were a spoon?" or "How might I like to be different from other spoons?" The procedure is a deliberate attempt to promote personal involvement.

A *compressed conflict* is produced through a deliberate attempt to bring about deferment. It often involves attempting to think of the exact opposite of what has been the focus of one's attention. The *compressed conflict* is realized when two seemingly opposite words are fused into one statement. The resultant product may, at first, seem like a pair of mutually exclusive terms, but likely provokes a unique image. One example cited by Gordon and Poze is "Bulky Precision." The referent for this *compressed conflict* is an elephant picking up a peanut. Another is "Lifesaving Destroyer." Here the referent is fire for a person trapped in a blizzard. The metaphor may suggest to the inventor or problem solver whole new ways of seeing the problem and solutions to it.

The metaphor which appears to have the most direct bearing on the act of invention is the *direct analogy*. This is simply a comparison between two objects which, if perceptively viewed, share something in common. The commonalities are not always readily apparent, but an astute observer forcing the analogy may discern in the counterpoint situation or behavior a clue which leads to new opportunities or to the solution of his or her own problem. Invention history is replete with examples of such analogous imaginging and thinking. The following, extracted from Gordon and Poze and from the author's own reading on the subjects of invention and inventors, illustrate the point.

Velcro was invented by an engineer who astutely noted the clinging properties of the burrs which stuck to his clothing when he went on walks through fields.

Pringles potato chips were invented when an employee carefully noted that wet leaves falling from trees did not crumble as did leaves which were dry when they fell. The inventive employee noted an analogy and new product invention was born. Potatoes were sliced wet and then dried.

R. Buckminster Fuller began to observe nature as the source for his invention ideas at a very young age. He was only nine years old when, after careful observation of marine life, he invented a mechanical jellyfish to propel his boat through the Maine coastal waters. Later observing tiny, microscopic marine protozoa, Fuller noted that nature's basic building block is the tetrahedron. He patterned his geodesic domes on a model observed first in nature.

Orville and Wilbur Wright had difficulty stabilizing the wings of their aircraft while turning. Carefully noting how buzzards twisted the tips of their wings in flight, the Wright brothers made a creative connection. Control wires were linked to flaps on the wings to stabilize the flight of their airplane.

Alexander Graham Bell came from a family which had scientifically studied speech and hearing for three generations. He patterned the telephone after the natural working mechanism of the human ear.

Camouflage, used by the military, has always been a vital ingredient in nature's scheme of things.

The following quotation seems especially appropriate to share with students when discussing the above examples and the use of the tool of *direct analogy.*

> Before he can create, man must have a deep awareness of the world
> about him — he must be able to really see, hear, feel, touch, and move.
> —Harold A. Rothbart

The use of Synectics, especially the *direct analogy*, appears to be a highly appropriate tool for young inventors to employ as they search for new combinations, especially in the *imagination* phase of inventing. Once students have identified the problem they want to solve, they may next wish to search for situations in nature which are analogous to their chosen problem. How does nature solve the problem? To note an example cited earlier, scientists are no doubt today considering how they can emulate the polar bear and increase the efficiency of solar heating power.

Ask students to imagine what inventors, designers, and engineers may have learned from bats, flying squirrels, migrating birds, dolphins, and kangaroos. Students may also benefit from playing the game of "animal crackers." What answers can students give to the following probes? Name nature's counterparts to:

Sherlock Holmes

a fisherman

a hospital worker

a computer

a butler

a bank guard or a banker

a thief in the night

a conceited movie star

a hang glider

a traffic controller (air and/or ground)

a life guard

a plumber

a hair dresser

an opera singer

an attorney

Though the activity is primarily lighthearted, the connections students make might suggest further connections which may be important to their search for new inventions.

WHAT TO INVENT?

Conventional wisdom dictates that writers should write about things with which they are familiar. This generalization seems to carry over to the process of inventing as well. People invent solutions to problems which are found in their primary environments. Consider the case of women inventors. It is not sexist to note that a very large number of the patents held by women are for domestic inventions: sewing and washing machine improvements, mops, sweepers, irons, etc. Clothing improvements and cosmetics are also areas in which women hold many patents. But, recall from the earlier discussion of women inventors that they became creators of arms and munitions-related inventions during World War I. Why? Historically, in times of war women have contributed significantly to the production of arms and munitions. They have had access to factories, machines, tools, and skills which had previously been off limits to them. Once women became familiar with the field of arms and munitions, then they began to invent within its domain. Women have also been inventors in the agricultural domain because it is another arena in which they have toiled. In states where they have shared farming with their husbands and brothers, women have invented plows, grain and grass mowers, and other farm-related equipment.[15]

The old saying states that "Familiarity breeds contempt," but it also no doubt facilitates understanding of problems and needs. Inventors create tools and processes to improve environments in which they live and work. For students, familiar environments are most probably school and home. In *Mothers of Invention*, authors Ethlie Ann Vare and Greg Ptacek relate the story of how Becky Schroeder conceived the idea for the Glo-Sheet when she was ten. One evening Miss Schroeder accompanied her mother while she ran errands. Sitting in the parked family car thinking about her homework which needed to be completed, she wondered why there was not some way to write in the dark. It occurred to her there might be a way to illuminate the paper, and she was on the way to inventing the Glo-Sheet, for which she earned her first patent. The inventor had worked on a problem, school homework, which stemmed from one of her primary environments, school.[16]

A point of caution to share with students beginning to invent is to work within environments with which they are familiar. Typically, student inventions might be related to school, home, and recreational environments. This does not preclude the exception where a student has an unusually high level of familiarity with another environment. For example, a young person who has been involved in a family business since childhood may well have considerable expertise *and* motivation to invent within that arena.

In an excellent article in *The Elementary School Journal*, B. Edward Shlesinger, Jr. makes an interesting point about invention projects in the classroom:

> It is important that all the children in a class work on the same project so that they can compare notes. Observation has disclosed that children work better and more competitively when they are assigned the same tool to develop rather than when each is assigned a different tool.[17]

Shlesinger goes on to point out that this suggested procedure does not prohibit students from individually working on other, separate inventions. While learning the *process* of inventing, however, he recommends that all students have the same invention task.

Factors such as the age of students, geography, program goals, and the classroom subject matter focus will determine what teachers ask students to invent. Regardless, the invention focus should take into account the needs, interests, and environments with which students can identify and problem solve.

An early point of departure might involve an education-related toy or game. The author presented a fifth-grade class of students with a box of randomly chosen common items (e.g., rubber bands, paper clips, nuts and bolts, small blocks of scrap wood, old keys, string, pen caps) and asked each student to use the items plus any others they wanted to add to invent a game to teach a younger child a simple arithmetic function.

Some observations of the experiment are worth noting. A deadline for completion was given. At first a lot of individual experimentation occurred. However, if students did not have a fixed idea as the deadline approached, a sort of panic developed, and with it experimentation stopped and imitation took over. That is, students did not copy and steal other's ideas until the end of the time period approached. Invention does not occur according to the dictates of the calendar or stop watch. Pressuring students to meet a particular deadline may not serve as the motivation force intended. Rather, it more likely will induce imitation.

Observation of the students also led to the belief that there is a very fine line between purposeful experimentation and playing around with ideas and just plain goofing off. An outside observer might have perceived that students were wasting time when, in fact, the students were quite consciously and deliberately experimenting with new designs. Another observation was that the technical input, the lesson in simple physics, for example, may not always be most valuable at the front end of the lesson sequence. Students needed to work and experiment for a time and reach a point where they realized themselves that they had need of new information and skills.

A final observation of the students and the work produced is important. Which is the teacher's primary goal, process or product? The answer will largely dictate how one judges the students and the results. Initially, it seems vital to concentrate on the process. The first products students generate will not, in all likelihood, be remarkable in their novelty or perfection of design and operation. One of the problems with putting great emphasis on the product alone is that in order to achieve perfection the process may be sacrificed and the value of learning may be lost. This is seen too often in science fairs and other competitions. A winning entry may look very good, but may have been actually the design and work of someone other than the child. Meanwhile, some of the projects which look less than dazzling are the products of real and significant learning on the part of their creators. Making mistakes is a natural part of the learning process. It is vital to allow for magnificent failures as well as brilliant successes, especially if the former ultimately pay off in the end result.

WRITING ABOUT INVENTING AND INVENTIONS

The head of the chemistry division of a pharmaceutical company once told the author that he had reached a point in his hiring practice where, faced with choices between equally qualified young chemists for job openings in the company, he increasingly looked for candidates with good writing skills. "I do not have time to edit and rewrite my employees' reports," he said.

One of the spin-offs of inventing is the writing experience students gain. Often the writing of school-age students is unfocused and lacks precision. Writing which describes an invention must be both concise and precise. A stranger must be able to determine from a set of drawings *and words* exactly how a tool or process works. The stranger must be able to duplicate the results and replicate the process. Vital steps or parts cannot be left out of the description. Writing the text or copy to accompany drawings for an invention is excellent practice in clear communication for students.

As a point of practice, give students a relatively simple invention task. Examples might include the creation of a child's toy or a labor-saving device for teenagers which uses as its base a common item such as a coat hanger, paper clip, comb, styrofoam cup, spoon, or rubber band. Students may combine the first object with other items of choice. Emphasize the instructions, both written and visual.

When students have completed their inventions, ask them to assume the role of patent examiners. Students exchange inventions with one another. Each patent examiner silently reads the instructions the inventor has provided and determines whether or not the invention works. Inventors can provide no verbal explanations. The patent examiner's decisions is based entirely on his or her reading of the invention description and physical handling of the invention.

CREATIVE WRITING VENTURES

The creative writer is also an inventor of sorts. His or her tools are words and if so chosen, the writer legally protects his or her "invention" with a copyright. Numerous opportunities for creative writing stem from work with inventions. Some of these many possibilities are described in figure 4.4. For convenience of use with students, the language is directed toward them.

WRITING CREATIVELY ABOUT INVENTING, INVENTIONS, AND INVENTORS

1. Write an ode or an essay celebrating the accomplishments of a great inventor, or a class of inventors (e.g., aviation inventors, women inventors, children and adolescent inventors).

2. Write a story about a young inventor. The plot might be about how the youthful inventor solves a problem which has school authorities baffled, or about how the young inventor struggles to receive recognition for his or her invention.

3. Write a serious or funny story in which the theme is related to one of the famous sayings or quotations about invention. For example, what plot line might evolve out of consideration of the proverb: "Necessity is the Mother of Invention." Perhaps a humorous story could evolve out of such a saying if it is given a funny twist. What might the plot be for a story with the title, "Invention is the Necessity of My Mother!"

4. "Uncle Sam Needs You!" and "A mind is a terrible thing to waste" are extremely powerful slogans that have been invented by people. Invent a slogan which represents something fine to say about an issue or cause in which you believe. Design a poster to show off the slogan to its best effect. Send both the poster and slogan to the appropriate agency.

5. Create an autobiography for an invention. Using the writing tool of personification, pretend to be the Model T or the telephone or even an Oreo cookie. Tell the highs and lows of your life story.

6. Invent a new subject or discipline which you believe should be taught in school. Write a syllabus for the unit or course of instruction. Also, write a statement for a school board meeting at which you would propose adoption of the new course.

7. Christmas ornaments made of dough appear to be a relatively new invention which has become very popular. Perhaps you can create a new craze. Think of some common, everyday ingredients and products which could be given new application and use. Write an article about your new product or process invention for *Popular Mechanics, Better Homes and Gardens* or another popular magazine.

(Fig. 4.4 continues on page 88.)

Fig. 4.4—*Continued*

8. Describe a mousetrap, but do not draw any pictures or diagrams which illustrate the conceived invention. Exchange papers with a classmate. Each person draws a picture of the proposed mousetrap based on the written directions. No verbal exchange or questions may be asked. How effective were the instructions? Do the resultant drawings convey the image the original author/inventor conceived? Now, pass the instructions and drawing to a third person. Ask that person to build a replica of the mousetrap without benefit of any verbal questions or commands.

9. Choose an invention or invention category and write an acrostic poem similar to the following celebration of robots.

   Rossum's Unlimited Robots (R.U.R.)

   Odex I

   Bionic

   One in every classroom by _____?

   Teachers? Tutors?

   Satellite station servicebots?

10. Not all inventions are technical or mechanical. Create, design, and invent a new dust jacket for a favorite book. Create a new game for children to play on board a space vehicle destined for Mars. The journey will take a long time so the children need a game which will entertain them for extended periods of time, yet will require few tools or tokens and can be played on board. Invent a new dessert to be served on picnics. Write a new school song. Invent a code for spies to use in a time of war. Invent a new number system.

11. Create a want ad for an inventor. What qualities should applicants possess? What are the benefits of the job?

Fig. 4.4. A student handout.

CREATIVE THINKING EXERCISES

Sometimes a class needs a two-minute opening shot in the arm as a motivator. On other occasions, the planned lesson ends five minutes before the class period is over. The following creative prompts are short and make great fillers when an entire lesson is not needed, but something other than idleness is the desired outcome.

1. Tomato juice is famed for its many supposed cures such as getting rid of skunk odors. Invent a new use for tomato juice. Describe the procedure of usage. How might word of the new discovery be spread?

2. Invent a new slogan to encourage tourism in the city or state. Conversely, what slogan might keep pesky tourists at a distance?

3. List 10 inventive uses for old newspapers.
   List 10 things one can make with old calendars.
   List 10 inventive things one could do with old tires.
   List 5 new uses for old lamp shades.
   List 10 new uses for a birdbath.
   List 10 uses for snow tires in Hawaii.
   List 10 uses for a surfboard in Alaska.

4. Invent a new line of greeting cards. What might be the central gimmick or appeal? Cards will be needed for weddings, graduations, birthdays, etc. How will the theme carry across the many events for which there are greeting cards?

5. Invent a new soft drink. What accounts for its uniqueness? Suggest a slogan or jingle for the advertising of the product.

6. Something dreadful has happened at the U.S. Patent Office. An entire carton of pending patents has been inadvertly destroyed. Only the names of the inventions remain (they were listed on a manifest which was not destroyed). Be creative and reinvent these now-missing inventions:

   a homework machine which guarantees straight As

   a bedroom mess picker-upper

   a mechanical school lunch room supervisor

   an "I'm grounded" home entertainment center

   an envelope and stamp licker

7. Invent a "thingamabob" which uses all six simple machines. The resultant contraption may be used for any task or leisure activity.

8. Invent a device or process which will keep an ice cube frozen for the longest time possible.

9. Invent a procedure or device which will arrest the speed at which a ball bearing or marble released from a height of three feet will reach the ground. Have a running contest to see which student can, over the course of the school year, achieve the slowest drop time.

10. Consider the possible applications of the technology devised in activity 9. After brainstorming lots of possibilities, select one of the best uses of the slow drop procedure and give a creative sales pitch to probable buyers.

11. The chief executive officer (CEO) of one of the nation's largest automobile manufacturers has put out a call for designs for a new super sports car. The new sports car must have a new look, and must feature a design which is aerodynamically efficient. Design a sports car which meets these criteria. Draw the vision of the sports car from several angles: front, back, and side. If the automobile has special hood ornaments or other identifying emblems, these should also be featured in the portfolio to be created for the automobile company CEO.

12. A grand and magnificent Egyptian pharaoh has hired you to create a tamperproof pyramid to protect his gems and golden statues. Invent a security system to protect the pharaoh's tomb.

13. Michelle Alexander was nine year old when she invented the "Give Peace a Chance" board game. She has played the game with world leaders like Andrei Gromyko, and her game has been translated into several foreign languages, including Russian. Emulate Michelle's inventive behavior. Create a board game which invites players to consider a significant issue such as the conservation of wildlife and natural resources or the importance of volunteerism and service to humanity.

INVENTION BACKPACKS

Take the boring, lethargic, no-work monkey off the backs of gifted students and substitute invention backpacks. What is an invention backpack? It is a transportable, minilearning center packaged in a backpack or bookbag. The backpack is filled with library books and/or laminated reprints of book chapters, articles, and other print matter about inventions, inventors, and inventing, plus a set of activity cards for students to complete, *and* anything else creative teachers and school library media specialists prepare. Students then check out the backpacks from the classroom or library and complete a desired number of activities overnight or over a weekend.

Laminated activity cards can be directed reading assignments. For example, a task card might ask students to read a chapter out of a book contained in the backpack about the life of Thomas Edison and answer six questions about his life and work. Each question represents a different level of Bloom's taxonomy.[18]

Knowledge:	Where was Edison born?
Comprehension:	Explain how Edison improved Alexander Graham Bell's telephone?
Application:	Survey your home. List all the items in your home for which Edison either invented or improved original models.
Analysis:	Thomas Edison was disabled. He suffered damage to his ears which made it impossible for him to hear ordinary conversation. In what ways was Edison's disability both an advantage and a disadvantage?
Synthesis:	Select one of the dramatic events in Edison's childhood. Pretend you are Edison at that moment in time, and write about this event in a diary he might have kept.
Evaluation:	Thomas Edison, Abraham Lincoln, George Washington, Teddy Roosevelt, John F. Kennedy, and Martin Luther King, Jr. are all very famous American figures from the past. Compare Edison to the others on this list. If you ranked these historical figures in order of importance to U.S. history, where would you rank Edison? Explain your ranking.

Other backpack activities can relate to any of the many skills and talents teachers want to address and emphasize: critical thinking exercises (substitute the names of inventors or inventions in classic logic puzzles), creative writing tasks, communication and planning activities, etc. While many activities for an invention backpack will require solitary reading, reflection, and writing, it may be well to include some action-oriented options for students. The topic of invention lends itself especially well to scientific experiments with electricity which can be performed easily and safely at home. The school library media center should be well supplied with science activity books which detail simple, safe electrical experiments.

It is a good idea to include at least one activity which will engage one parent or adult, if not the whole family. Perhaps the family can play a trivia game about inventors or participate in a conservation of energy scavenger hunt, either of which the student is directed to first create. A good problem solving activity could be the Smithsonian/Edison light bulb exercise cited earlier in this chapter or a variation: the egg drop packaging task. Ask each family member to creatively and inventively package a raw egg in such a fashion so that when it is dropped from a second story window or staircase, it will not break. At a grand family send off, all the packages are dropped. Then the packages are opened and the winners are those whose eggs did not crack or break. The winners get ice cream while the losers have to do the dishes (and clean up the raw egg mess).

Backpacks allow gifted students additional opportunities to continue work about inventions outside the classroom. They also may allow opportunities for families to experience some of the fun and excitement of the inventions unit which is going on at school. It is a wise idea to also include a bibliography in the backpack which students can keep for continued reading enjoyment and future reference.

The example discussed here accents Thomas Edison. The topics and activities for individual backpacks are unlimited. Additional topics of excellence might include backpacks about women inventors, robots, aviation inventions, minority inventors, the invention of toys, inventing toys and games for holidays, and weird and funny inventions. The teacher or school library media specialist does not have to be the only inventor of invention backpacks. Students can receive extra credit for creating invention backpacks for other students to use. Parent volunteers might also be enlisted to create invention backpacks for the classroom and the library.

PATENTS

It is not the function of this text to provide an extensive discussion of how patents are obtained. The discussion of patent applications and procedures is exceptionally well covered in resources which will be mentioned below. Also, given the financial expense and time investment needed to secure a patent, it is rather unlikely that most school-age students will pursue this course of action. Joanne Mordus of Affiliated Inventors Foundation, a national organization created to assist inventors, estimates the average cost of obtaining a standard patent at $3,000.00. The cost represents fees for searches, applications, and patent attorney fees. The costs of product development and testing are *not* included in the estimate. Mordus also states that the minimal time expended to obtain a patent is two years.[19]

Numerous resources may be consulted which provide vital information about securing patents. All have been previously cited under "Resources" in the introductory chapter. Certainly, one of the initial print resources which should be tapped is an inexpensive booklet provided by the Patent and Trademark Office of the U.S. Department of Commerce. *General Information Concerning Patents* is a 41-page booklet which defines a patent, prescribes what kinds of inventions qualify for patents, the steps and procedures for obtaining a patent, and procedures for maintenance of the patent. A final section poses some of the most common questions asked about patents, and provides authoritive answers.

Works previously cited which include salient information about patents include the books *How to Invent*, by B. Edward Shlesinger, Jr., and *Steven Caney's Invention Book*, and the fine article *Dreams, Schemes, and 3,300 Mousetraps*, about the daily operations of the U.S. Patent Office, by Penny Ward Moser.

It may profit students to simulate the patent procedure through the completion of an invention record. The Record of Invention in figure 4.5 is duplicated here with permission of Affiliated Inventors. The completion of the record is one of the early steps Affiliated Inventors recommend inventors take in the patenting process.

When the subject of patents and procedures for obtaining one comes up, it may be an ideal time to invite a patent attorney to class to speak to students directly about the legal side of inventing. Patent attorneys are listed as such in the yellow pages of most telephone books. The local chapter of the American Bar Association should also be able to identify local patent attorneys who may be willing to speak to student groups.

The future lawyers in the class may want to become the classroom experts on current patent law. They may also want to research and enlighten the rest of the class about famous cases in patent history. Nikola Tesla's claim to the invention of the radio, for example, was supported by the U.S. Supreme Court a few months following his death. There have been many famous legal cases about trademarks as well as patents.

(Text continues on page 97.)

AFFILIATED
INVENTORS

AFFILIATED INVENTORS
FOUNDATION, INC.
2132 E. BIJOU STREET
COLORADO SPRINGS, CO 80909-5950
(719) 635-1234

Please turn to the back page for instructions on how to complete this form.

RECORD OF INVENTION

Be it known that I (we) _____

residing at _____
                              (Street)

_____
   (City)   (State)   (Zip)

have invented certain new and useful improvements in

_____
                         (Name of Invention)

as fully described and illustrated hereinafter.

   I first conceived the idea _____ .
                                         (date)

   I made my first sketch and description _____ .
                                                   (date)

   I made my first model (if any) _____ .
                                            (date)

                      _____
                                   (Signature)

Be it known that _____

has this day _____ of _____ , 19____ , disclosed to me (us) the invention

which is described and illustrated in the Record of Invention form. He calls his invention a

_____

and I (we) fully understand its construction, purpose and use.
            (Do not use members of the family or relatives as witnesses.)

Witness: _____   Address:_____

Witness: _____   Address: _____

101   Rev 2-88

(Fig. 4.5 continues on page 94.)

Fig. 4.5—*Continued*

USE THIS SPACE TO MAKE YOUR DRAWINGS

Use additional pages, as necessary.

PLEASE DESCRIBE YOUR INVENTION BELOW IN YOUR OWN WORDS

Name of Invention: _____

Model Available? Yes ___ No ___ (Please check one)

_____

_____

_____

_____

_____

_____

_____

_____

_____

_____

_____

_____

_____

_____

_____

_____

_____

_____

_____

_____

Use additional pages, as necessary.

3

(Fig. 4.5 continues on page 96.)

Fig. 4.5—*Continued*

INSTRUCTIONS

1. Complete pages 2 and 3. On page 2, your sketch need not be a finished drawing. Appearance is not important at this stage as long as we can understand your invention. You will find it easier to explain your invention if you assign numbers to the parts.

2. In the written description of your invention on page 3, tell how it works, preferably by reference to part numbers shown on the sketch. Also, do include the advantages your invention possesses. Please print or write clearly.

3. If the space provided for drawings and description is not sufficient, use additional pages as necessary; however, be sure to have each of these additional pages signed and dated by your witnesses.

4. After completing the sketch and description (pages 2 and 3), have one or two (your option) witnesses complete the bottom section on the cover page. **Do not use members of the family or relatives as witnesses.**

5. Complete the top portion on page 1, keeping the dates confidential.

6. While steps 1 through 4 are the preferable procedure, a notary public may be used as an alternative witness. Simply have him or her complete the certificate at the bottom of this page.

7. After completing this form, you should keep it in a safe place and it should not be shown to others. If it is necessary to disclose the details of your invention to others for business purposes, photocopy the inside pages (2 and 3) ONLY. No one other than your attorney in a future legal action needs to know the dates or names of your witnesses on pages 1 or 4.

CERTIFICATE OF NOTARY PUBLIC

State of _____

County of _____

}§

I, _____
being duly sworn, depose and say: That I am
the person who invented the device illustrated and described herein.

Subscribed and sworn to before me this _____ day of _____ 19_____

NOTARY PUBLIC _____

My commission expires _____

NOTARIAL
SEAL
HERE

Fig. 4.5. Record of Invention form. Courtesy Affiliated Inventors.

In a similar fashion, the classroom economists may want to examine the economic side of patents and trademarks and the marketing of inventions. This is an equally fascinating field of inquiry. *Breakthroughs* by Nayak and Ketteringham is perhaps the best contemporary resource. Various business magazines and *The Wall Street Journal* will also feature stories about national and global competition.

NOTES

[1]Glenn S. Grow, "Cozy in the Cold: The Polar Bear's Solar Secret," *Christian Science Monitor* (1 December 1987): 19.

[2]Additional resource material on polar bears was taken from "Polar Bears," *Zoo Books* 5, no. 2 (San Diego, Calif.: Wildlife Federation, Inc., 1987).

[3]B. Edward Shlesinger, Jr., "Teaching Problem Solving through Invention," *Vocational Education Journal* 62, no. 5 (August 1987): 26.

[4]Isaac Asimov, *Asimov's Biographical Encyclopedia of Science and Technology*, 2nd rev. ed. (Garden City, N.Y.: Doubleday & Company, Inc., 1982), 561.

[5]B. Edward Shlesinger, Jr., *How to Invent: A Text for Teachers and Students* (New York: IFI/Plenum Data Corporation, 1987). Shlesinger's work is also available in a video. For complete details, contact IFI/Plenum Data Corporation, 302 Swann Avenue, Alexandria, VA 22301.

[6]Ruth B. Noller, Sidney J. Parnes, and Angelo M. Biondi, *Creative Actionbook* (New York: Charles Scribner's Sons, 1976).

[7]*Creative Problem Solving: How to Get Better Ideas*, CRM Films, 1979. For complete details about this film, its rental or purchase, contact CRM Films, 2233 Faraday Avenue, Suite F, Carlsbad, CA 92008, 800-421-0833.

[8]Charles E. Wales and Robert Stager, *Guided Design* (Morgantown, W. Va.: University of West Virginia Department of Engineering, 1977), 14.

[9]This grid was completed by the author based upon work done by his former students in the Kalamazoo, Michigan Public Schools, who participated in the National Future Problem Solving Program in 1979, 1980.

[10]Noller et al., 159-60.

[11]P. Ranganath Nayak and John M. Ketteringham, *Breakthroughs* (New York: Rawson Associates, 1986): 14.

[12]Bob Eberle, *Visual Thinking: A SCAMPER Tool for Using Imaging* (East Aurora, N.Y.: D.O.K. Publishers, 1982); Alex F. Osborn, *Applied Imagination: Principles and Procedures for Creative Problem Solving* (New York: Charles Scribner's Sons, 1961).

[13]Don Koberg and Jim Bagnall, *The All-New Universal Traveler* (Los Altos, Calif.: William Kaufmann, Inc., 1976), 72.

[14]W. J. J. Gordon and Tony Poze, *The Metaphorical Way of Learning and Knowing* (Cambridge, Mass.: SES Associates, 1979). *See also*: W. J. J. Gordon and Tony Poze, *Strange & Familiar* (Cambridge, Mass.: SES Associates, 1972).

[15]Fred Amram, "The Innovative Woman," *New Scientist* 1411 (May 24, 1984): 10-12.

[16]Ethlie Ann Vare and Greg Ptacek, *Mothers of Invention: From the Bra to the Bomb: Forgotten Women & Their Unforgettable Ideas* (New York: William Morrow & Company, Inc., 1988), 245-46.

[17]B. Edward Shlesinger, Jr., "An Untapped Resource of Inventors: Gifted and Talented Children," *Elementary School Journal* 82, no. 3 (January 1982): 218.

[18]The factual questions in the quiz are based on information derived from *Thomas Edison: The Great American Inventor* by Louise Evans from the series *Solutions: Profiles in Science for Young People* (New York: Barron's Educational Series, Inc., 1987).

[19]Conversation with Joanne Mordus, Affiliated Inventors Foundation, Colorado Springs, Colorado, June 1988.

5

A Digression
A Look at the Humorous Side of Inventions, Inventors, and Inventing

Anyone who has ever worked with gifted adolescents knows that one characteristic many of these students share is a wacky sense of humor. The gifted student often appreciates *and* creates humor which is beyond the comprehension of his or her less gifted classmates. Gifted students enjoy puns which may go undetected by their age peers. They love humor which has a scientific basis. (They are not alone. Gary Larson, creator of "The Far Side," counts scientists and engineers among his biggest fans.) The class wit may well find a creative outlet in an invention unit which focuses on humor. Many possibilities exist.

CARTOONS

Cartoonists love inventors and their inventions as subjects. They delight in showing us what happens when inventions do not work the way they are supposed to, in portraying the mad inventor in his laboratory, or in humorously presenting a version of the "Eureka!" experience. Encourage students to create cartoons about specific inventions, the inventing process, or great moments in the lives of famous inventors. The following might be possible starting ideas:

1. Illustrate why a particular invention is especially vexing.

2. Depict a famous event in an inventor's life in a comic manner (e.g., young Edison's chemical fire aboard the train on which he worked).

3. Convey humorously what life might be like without a particular invention.

4. Create the opposite of a famous invention (e.g., the "dark" bulb rather than the light bulb).

5. Portray an inventor's reaction to a experiment failure (e.g., Wilbur and Orville Wright's flight that did *not* succeed).

6. Show the reaction a 19th century inventor might have to 1980's usage of his or her invention (e.g., how might Edison view today's movies?).

7. Portray a caveman's reaction to his discovery or invention of something basic such as the wheel.

8. Illustrate a great new invention such as a rib-tickler, spine-tingler, or foot-stomping machine.

RUBE GOLDBERG INVENTIONS

Gadgets and contraptions of all kinds were the forte of Rube Goldberg, whose cartoons have delighted Americans for much of the 20th century. Goldberg began his career as a sports cartoonist for a San Francisco newspaper and then moved on to New York where he drew daily cartoons for the *Evening Mail*. He created his first invention cartoon in 1914. He described his wacky invention cartoons as "symbols of man's capacity for exerting maximum effort to accomplish minimal results."[1] His drawings delight us because he pokes fun at our ridiculous penchant for more often than not taking the hard rather than easy and obvious path to solving problems. He also touches a sensitive nerve in the national psyche: our nagging doubt about whether or not modern science and technology really do make life better. Should we always believe those geniuses who tell us to trust in science? Goldberg was awarded the Pulitzer prize in 1948.

No student should study the inventions of the modern era without taking time to look at Goldberg's cartoons. One excellent compilation is *The Best of Rube Goldberg* by Charles Keller. Figure 5.1 is an example of Goldberg's wonderful wit.[2] Figure 5.2 is a Rube Goldberg-style invention by student Adam Burton, the illustrator of this book.

Imitation is the sincerest form of flattery, and the Goldberg style has been copied often. For years, British humorist David E. H. Jones has written a humor column in the magazine *New Scientist* under the pen name of Daedalus. The allusion is to the Greek mythological inventor who might be called the father of aviation. Jones's inventions test the limits of science in a humorous fashion. He may ask, for example, why humans have not invented ways to amplify smell in the same way they have invented telescopes and microphones to amplify, respectively, sight and sound. He is then off and running with a wild invention description, complete with highly scientific terms, explanations, and schematics. *The Inventions of Daedalus: A Compendium of Plausible Schemes* is a collection of 129 of the best Daedalus columns which students gifted in the sciences will love to read. Most of Jones's inventions find their way to DREADCO (Daedalus Research, Evaluation, And Development Corporation) for testing and development.[3]

American scientists did Deadalus one better. Rather than just have a column devoted to invention humor, American scholars created an entire journal devoted to scientific nonsense. Edited by Dr. George H. Scherr, *The Journal of Irreproducible Results* is a compilation of some of the best tongue-in-cheek proposals, schemes, and inventions of American scientists. A mechanical-portable elephant, the darkbulb, and no-fault crime insurance are just a few of the wild concoctions of scientists who have taken breaks from their laboratories to wreak havoc in the field of invention literature with their immodest proposals. Again, gifted young science students will delight in this nonsense. One should be cautioned that while the contents are certainly not pornographic, the scientists are writing for their peers and the humor is occasionally adult in nature. Wise teachers will be selective in the use of this fun resource.[4]

Automatic Sheet Music Turner

At last! The great brain of the distinguished man of science gives the world the simple automatic sheet music turner!

Press left foot (**A**) on pedal (**B**) which pulls down handle (**C**) on tire pump (**D**). Pressure of air blows whistle (**E**)–goldfish (**F**) believes this is dinner signal and starts feeding on worm (**G**). The pull on string (**H**) releases brace (**I**), dropping shelf (**J**), leaving weight (**K**) without support. Naturally, hatrack (**L**) is suddenly extended and boxing glove (**M**) hits punching bag (**N**) which, in turn, is punctured by spike (**O**).

Escaping air blows against sail (**P**) which is attached to page of music (**Q**), which turns gently and makes way for the next outburst of sweet or sour melody.

Fig. 5.1. From the book *The Best of Rube Goldberg*, compiled by Charles Keller, © 1979. Used by permission of the publisher, Prentice-Hall, Inc., Englewood Cliffs, N.J.

THE SUPER MOUSE TRAP

The woman (1) steps on stool (2) to get away from mouse. The stool presses down on the springboard (3) that is stuck to the knife (4) which cuts the rope (5) which drops weight (6) on one end of the board (7). The other end of the board flips on the fan (8) which blows the two squirrels (9) off their resting places. They take the bags of nuts (10) off the scales (11) which lightens one end and drops the cage (12) onto the mouse (13).

Fig. 5.2. A Rube Goldberg-type invention, designed and illustrated by student Adam Burton. Used with permission.

In addition to simply enjoying the drawings and writing mentioned above, students can create their own wacky inventions and schemes. What modern-day tasks and institutions can they satirize? Would life really be so disastrous without the remote control television channel changer? What simple tasks in their own world of experience can they make more complicated with witty inventions? Perhaps the idea can evolve into a class project. For example, each student might create a Goldberg-style invention for students or for the classroom which could become part of a classroom catalog of bizarre school supplies and needs. The class might also produce its own version of the *Journal of Irreproducible Results* with humorous pseudoscience research papers and essays about new inventions and experiments with new ways to utilize existing inventions. For example, an experiment is set up to determine if too many cooks spoil the broth remains a truthful adage in an era of microwave ovens and food processors.

REAL INVENTIONS THAT ARE/WERE BIZARRE

To receive a patent, an invention is supposed to meet the criteria of being new, workable, and useful. An examination of some of the four million patents awarded in the history of the U.S. Patent Office suggests that occasionally the patent examiners have been, to say the least, lenient in their interpretation of the usefulness criterion. Eyeglasses for chickens, an upper lip shaping device, a tapeworm trap, and an illumination device to be worn by cats to frighten mice away are among the more bizarre items to receive patents from the patent office in its nearly 200 years of history. Figure 5.3 is an example of one such patented invention. It is reprinted from the delightful *Absolutely Mad Inventions* by A. E. Brown and H. A. Jeffcott, Jr.[5] In addition to the Brown and Jeffcott book another excellent collection of wild and bizarre inventions which were not intentionally humorous and *really* did receive patents is Kenneth Lasson's *Mousetraps and Muffling Cups: One Hundred Brilliant and Bizarre U.S. Patents* (New York: Arbor House Publishing Co., 1986).

In addition to examining these real, but weird inventions, students can write humorous stories about how different life might be today if these inventions had not withered away into obscurity, but had become indispensible facets of everyday life, past and present.

Hat without Headaches

UNITED STATES PATENT OFFICE

HAT

1,045,060   Specification of Letters Patent   Patented Nov. 19, 1912
Application filed May 10, 1911. Serial No. 626,282

. . . The objects of the invention are, to provide a hat which will permit of free circulation of air entirely around and over the head of the wearer, thus to prevent headaches caused by the weight and close fitting of the ordinary hat; to allow free movements of the head of the wearer independently of the hat; to afford unobstructed exhibition of the ornamentation and trimming of the wearer's hair and of the hat; to remove all weight from the head and transfer it to the shoulders of the user; to render it possible to employ a hat of such size as to avoid the use of a parasol or umbrella, and yet not in any way inconvenience the user by an added weight of material; to adapt a hat to be constructed of any material desired, such, for instance, as waterproof fabric, whereby to extend the range of its usefulness; to construct the article in such manner as to render it at once light, cheap and durable; and in general, to furnish a novel and thoroughly practical article of head-wear. . . .

For storm use, a rubber bag or covering may be employed, which may be placed over the exterior of the hat, or the frame itself may be covered with a waterproof material and thus provide an effective shield against moisture. . . .

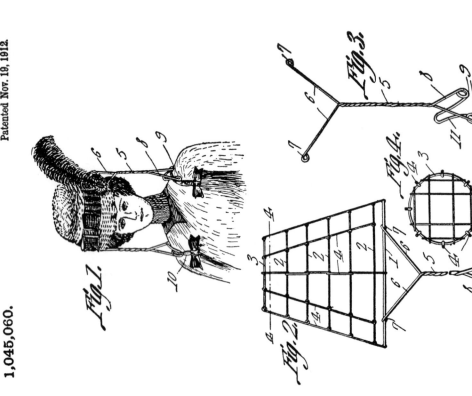

Fig. 5.3. From *Absolutely Mad Inventions* by A. E. Brown and H. A. Jeffcott, Jr., © 1970.
Reprinted with permission from the publisher, Dover Publications, Mineola, N.Y.

FOOLING AROUND WITH HISTORY
AND OTHER STUFF

Suppose the fairy godmothers had been on strike when Cinderella needed one the most, or that the woodsman had been home sick with the flu on that fateful day when the wolf showed up at Little Red Riding Hood's grandmother's cottage. What could these two damsels in distress have done if faced with such problems? Ask students if they can create inventions to assist famed fairy tale and folklore characters to deal with their travails. If students need a prompt, use the creative thinking technique of forced associations, randomly choosing 5 or 10 items which must be worked into whatever invention they create. For example, ask students to create a wolf-slaying device which could be utilized by Little Red Riding Hood should the axe-bearing woodsman be on vacation the day she visits grandmother with a basket of goodies. The wolf-slayer must use, among other things:

a pitcher of water	a back scratcher	Tinker toys
a key chain	a bird cage	a police whistle
an eggbeater	a boomerang	

For extra fun, have students pantomime how their invention will work after they have designed it.

"A horse! a horse! my kingdom for a horse!" (*King Richard III*, Act V, Scene IV). According to Shakespeare, all was lost for poor King Richard due to the unavailability of a horse. How might King Richard have saved his kingdom if he had been more inventive? Ask students to humorously rewrite history by coming up with inventions to help famous historical figures in their darkest hours.

A final thought about humor. Students can explore societal values and philosophical issues related to humor and comedy and the roles they and their creators play in society. Are not the comic, cartoonist, and humorist inventors? If so, in what way? What value do they contribute? Which is the greater invention for the benefit of humanity—a funny story or a nuclear bomb? Why? Do we underappreciate the role of inventive humorists in our society?

NOTES

[1]Keller, Charles, comp., *The Best of Rube Goldberg* (Englewood Cliffs, N.J.: Prentice-Hall, Inc., 1979), xii.

[2]*Ibid*, 53.

[3]David E. H. Jones, *The Inventions of Daedalus: A Compendium of Plausible Schemes* (San Francisco: W. H. Freeman & Company, 1982).

[4]George H. Scherr, ed., *The Journal of Irreproducible Results: Improbable Investigations and Unfounded Findings* (New York: Workman Publishing Company, Inc., 1983).

[5]A. E. Brown and H. A. Jeffcott, Jr., *Absolutely Mad Inventions* (Dover Publications, Inc., 1970), 16-17.

6

The Future

If there is a central characteristic besides sheer genius which is most commonly associated with the lives of the great inventors and discoverers, it is that they have always been men and women of *vision*. Inventors like Nikola Tesla and Alexander Graham Bell dreamed of worlds their contemporaries could not even imagine. An integral part of any study of inventors should be future studies. What are tomorrow's possibilities? What kind of lives will the children and grandchildren of today's students experience? It is important for young people to not only have the skills and talents to be inventive, it is vital that they be encouraged to dream. George Bernard Shaw expressed the thought beautifully when he said, "Some men see things as they are and ask 'Why?' I dream of things that never were and ask, 'Why not?'" Young gifted students, capable of so much promise for themselves and humanity, must be inspired to dream of great tomorrows. The future demands nothing less.

PEERING INTO THE FUTURE OF INVENTIONS

Build upon the work students have done with time lines by asking them to extrapolate from the present and hypothesize future inventions. One futures technique that works well and is most appropriate in a unit about inventions is to look at all the inventions and items associated with a particular place or activity across several generations. For example, students might select automobile transportation as the topic of consideration. They would next find pictures of automobiles which their grandparents might have driven at a given age such as sixteen. Next, they would locate examples of cars which their parents could have driven while in high school. This is followed with contemporary examples of transportation which are available. Finally, having examined artifacts from two past generations plus their own cars, they design automobiles their children and even their grandchildren will drive when they reach the same age.

Similar investigations could be made of school furniture and supplies, kitchen appliances, air travel, games and amusements, and communications media.

TRENDS AND TRENDING

Futurists study existing trends in order to predict possible and probable future events. They ask questions about the origins of trends, the likelihood of quick or gradual changes in the trends, and the current and probable consequences of trends. One example of a societal trend which has been worrisome to some observers is the increasing number of U.S. Patents awarded in the last decades to non-Americans. Does this trend mean Americans are losing the Yankee ingenuity which has been a national trademark? This particular trend is cited as one of the reasons the U.S. Patent Office has become a promoter of the *Weekly Reader* invention contest, the Invent America Program, and other invention contests.[1]

Historically, inventors have been followers and predictors of trends. As inventor/patent attorney/author B. Edward Shlesinger, Jr. points out in his suggested steps to inventing, inventors remain alert to problematic situations. Inventors look at trends and anticipate the new inventions the world needs to function within it or to overcome it.[2] Inventors today survey and note trends such as society's increasing need to find ways to dispose of its trash and proceed to invent tomorrow's waste disposal appliances and systems as well as reusable packages to cut down on waste products. Many shrewd inventors and business persons have noted that teens have more money today than in past generations. Inventors and entrepreneurs have been quick to find ways for young people to spend these excess funds. Others have noted that more and more people have greater amounts of leisure time and hence have turned their inventive talents to creating inventions people can use away from the work place. Some inventors noted the growth and proliferation of malls and created all kinds of equipment and services oriented in that direction.

Ask students to brainstorm observable trends in society today and potential trends they see on the horizon. Next, ask them to analyze the trends by posing who, what, how, where, why, and when questions about the proposed trends. Such questions will help students ascertain and anticipate probable needs which may be met with new inventions. Finally, ask students to be visionary inventors and to create inventions which will satisfy or meet the needs dictated by the hypothesized trends.

DELPHI POLLS

The oracle of Delphi gave predictions which were so convoluted they could be interpreted to have been prophetic regardless of actual outcomes. Although futurists like to believe their predictions are more reliable and trustworthy, they nonetheless have named one of their foremost information gathering tools after the Greek place of prophecy.

The first modern Delphi poll, conducted for the Air Force by the Rand Corporation, asked expert respondents to estimate how many atomic bombs the Russian military would need to destroy the munitions industry in the United States. Basically, a Delphi poll is an anonymous survey of experts through at least two rounds of questioning. In the second round, each respondent views the responses of others, who remain anonymous, and adjusts his or her answers if desired. The consensus ultimately achieved is believed to be more reliable than one reached through only one sampling. This may be in part due to the opportunity provided participants to rethink their original answer, especially when provided with data revealing what other experts in a field believe. Typically, the questions posed ask respondents to provide predictions of numbers and/or dates. Examples include:

By what date will someone have invented/discovered a vaccine to prevent cancer?

What percentage of patents granted in the year 2050 will be awarded to women?

Figure 6.1 is an example of a Delphi poll devoted to inventions. Students can design and conduct their own Delphi polls. First, they decide on the questions and options for answers they want to provide for respondents. Next, they need to decide who the respondents will be and proceed with the first round of questions. (It is perhaps unlikely that students will have access to a large population of experts, but they can nonetheless conduct a poll to determine the predictions of average citizens.) The results should be tabulated and shared with all the respondents without revealing any identities. Students then ask the respondents if they wish to revise their original predictions based upon their analysis of the first results. The polling may stop here or can be recycled through yet another round of sharing results and further questions. Ultimately, the final results are tabulated and shared. Students might want to share their results in their own *Invention Times* or forward them to the local media for use in a feature story.

In addition to learning about people's attitudes and beliefs about possible future inventions, students are experiencing a valuable lesson in sampling techniques and research. The Delphi poll is used in government, business, and, occasionally, education. Doctoral candidates in universities sometimes use the Delphi poll to collect data for their dissertations.

Please note that the Delphi poll procedure requires a great deal of record keeping. Therefore, it is a splendid opportunity for a student gifted in computers to show his or her talent by writing a program for the Delphi poll which can keep records and tabulate data.

DELPHI POLL

PROPOSED INVENTION	DESIRABLE OR UNDESIRABLE	1990-2000	2001-2010	2011-2020	2021-2030	2031-2040	2041-2050
CLONES							
ROBOTIC TEACHERS							
BIOCHEMICALS TO REPRODUCE LOST OR DAMAGED LIMBS							
??????							

Fig. 6.1. Delphi poll for inventions. Based on a design found in Charles Whaley, *Futures Studies: Personal and Global Possibilities* (New York: Trillium Press, Inc., 1984), p. 52.

SCIENCE FICTION AND SCENARIOS

Anything one man can imagine, other men can make real.
—Jonathan Swift

Allowing for the sexism in his comment, one may still credit Swift with an excellent observation. Of course, science fiction literature is often inventive on two levels. Not only are the best science fiction authors, including such luminaries as Ursula Le Guin, Isaac Asimov, and Arthur C. Clarke, creative and inventive in their use of literary forms, they often inspire others to bring to technological fruition their literary inventions. More than a few scientists and inventors search science fiction not only for enjoyment, but for new ideas. Science fiction authors have often been quite visionary. In *Twenty Thousand Leagues under the Sea*, Jules Verne describes a submarine which uses electric lighting. Workers from the *Nautilus* walk on the ocean floor breathing with the benefit of aqualungs. In 1870 when Verne wrote this classic, none of these things actually existed. Arthur C. Clarke wrote about synchronous communication satellites more than 20 years before they became a reality. Like many science fiction authors, he not only writes but is an active member of the scientific community. Many other examples of visionary thinking, past and present, may be found in science fiction literature. For excellent discussions of science fiction predictions, both right and wrong, direct students to these excellent resources:

Nicholls, Peter. *The Science in Science Fiction*. New York: Alfred A. Knopf, 1983.

Scholes, Robert, and Eric Rabkin. *Science Fiction: History, Science, Vision*. New York: Oxford University Press, 1978.

Most science fiction writers in the early decades of this century saw their writings published in pulp magazines like *Amazing Stories* and *Science Wonder Stories*. Some of the great illustrations originally used in science fiction magazines as well as in early issues of *Modern Mechanix* and *Popular Mechanics* magazines may be found in an excellent compendium, titled *Yesterday's Tomorrows: Past Visions of the American Future* by Joseph J. Corn and Brian Horrigan.[3]

There is another reason for including science fiction in a unit about inventions and inventing for gifted students. Science fiction and fantasy are far and away the most popular literary genre with gifted students, yet it receives very little critical study and exmination in the English and literature classes of most schools. In an encyclopedic, broad-based approach to the study of inventing, science fiction should certainly receive consideration. Students, working with the school library media specialist, may compile bibliographies of science fiction stories which feature special inventions and create a time line featuring real inventions which were first suggested via literature. Students can write critiques of science fiction stories and novels, paying particular attention to the feasibility of the inventions proposed. A lecture or slide-tape show might be orchestrated by one or more students using Peter Nicholls's *The Science in Science Fiction* as a prime resource.

As a follow-up on the activity of having students create original games (see chapter 2), have them design games which mix real and imagined inventors and inventions. Then have their classmates differentiate between the two groups. Many students will already be familiar with Captain Nemo's *Nautilus*, C3PO and R2-D2 from *Star Wars*, the computer HAL from *2001: A Space Odyssey*, and Dr. Frankenstein's terrible creation. Ask them to add other fictional inventors and inventions to their list as well as real inventors and inventions in the creation of their game.

Of course, students can write their own science fiction stories and novels based on products and services they envision for the future.

SCENARIOS

Less concerned with plot and character, but very much concerned with future inventions are scenarios. Scenarios are used in business and government to help people foresee what impact various technological, environmental, and societal changes will have. Figure 6.2, reprinted from *Writing Teacher* (February-March 1988), is the author's description of scenario writing as well as a project he created in his community. Of all the themes thus far posed in the described project, the invention theme has proved by far the most popular with students, especially in the middle and high school grades. Figures 6.3 (see page 116) and 6.4 (see page 120) are examples of scenarios written by students about their own visionary inventions and the impact they will have upon humanity. Both may be shared with students as examples of scenarios and for discussion about the feasibility of the proposed inventions. A natural extension of an inventions unit is to have students write scenarios about the impact of their own, or others, imagined future inventions.

(Text continues on page 123.)

INVENTING THE FUTURE:
WRITING ABOUT TOMORROW

The purpose of this article is to describe a joint education-business writing project which encourages young people to think about and describe the kinds of personal, national, and global futures we may have. It describes *scenario writing* which is a writing format new to most students.

INTRODUCTION

It has been said that what one person can envision, another can invent. It is probably unrealistic to suppose today's school-age youths should as yet be about the business of revolutionizing the world with their inventions. Few possess the engineering know-how to build tomorrow's tools today. It is not too soon, however, to ask young people to be visionaries, to use imagination and creativity to predict the marvels which may be commonplace in the next century. History provides confirmation of this belief. Yes, Einstein, Tesla, Edison, and the Wright brothers were doers, but they were first dreamers. Only when we help children dream and envision fantastic futures can such possibilities begin to emerge and take shape as probabilities.

A SCENARIO WRITING PROJECT

As a classroom teacher from 1966-1983, I grew ever more concerned with the growing pessimism about the future each new class of students expressed through their discussions and writings. Armed with the belief that it is essential for young people to have the opportunity to contemplate, examine, and explore their own images of the future, *and* have a forum in which to express such visions, I approached the major newspaper in my community with an idea: a jointly sponsored Scenario Writing Project for students K-12.

A scenario is a forecast of future events and conditions. Scenarios are written from the point-of-view of a future date. That is, a scenario written from the time perspective of 2010 is written in the present tense with all events leading up to 2010 referred to in the past tense. The scenario writer first envisions and then describes life as it *may* be in some future time. Scenarios differ from science fiction in that they are less concerned with plot and characterization and deal more with the typical and commonplace rather than the fantastic. For example, a scenario written in 1940 might have described a typical trip to the grocery store in the late 1980's and might have posited such notions as computer price code scanning and the availability of hydroponically grown produce.

The newspaper was enthusiastic and a partnership was born. Working cooperatively with the Newspaper In Education consultant at the Colorado Springs (CO) *Gazette-Telegraph*, a theme, a set of guidelines and rules, and judging procedures were established. The procedures outlined in the first year have worked well and have not been significantly altered. The newspaper widely advertises the project two or three times each week in daily editions of the newspaper during the fall months. The scenarios are due shortly before the school holiday recess in December. Scenarios are entered in four grade-level categories: K-3, 4-6, 7-9, 10-12. Judging occurs during January and February by university graduate students, retired school teachers, and journalists from the newspaper staff. The scenarios are evaluated holistically using the following criteria: readability and popular appeal; positivism of attitude or tone; grammar, spelling, and mechanics; and overall creativity and originality. Rules for the Scenario Writing Project are as follows:

Scenarios should not exceed 1,000 words in length.

Only one entry per student will be accepted.

All essays must be typed.

All writing must be the work of the student entrant.

The theme chosen the first year, "Images Of The Pikes Peak Region: 2001," accented both the region's dominant landmark and the futuristic thinking we wanted to encourage in students. Two hundred students responded to the challenge. The first-place scenarios in each of the four grade-level categories were prominently displayed on the front page of one section of the newspaper, and the public reaction to them was highly favorable. Overall, the writing was excellent and the technological marvels and inventions suggested by the students were exciting to contemplate. But the dominant impression of the future projected by the vast majority of the youth was dark and foreboding. Our most talented youth projected a future in which cities were domed because the atmosphere was too polluted to breathe. Tyrannical governments controlled not only speech and action, but thought as well. The spectre of nuclear war and annihilation was everpresent.

The second theme chosen for the Scenario Writing Project attempted to force the issue of positivism. "Welcome To The Future: Is It Going To Be A Great Place To Be" was purposefully chosen to direct the thinking of youth away from such dystopian future thinking. To further accentuate the positive a new component to the Scenario Writing Project, the Honors Convocation, was added the second year. The authors of the top 100 judged scenarios were invited to attend a spring Honors Convocation on the campus of the University of Colorado at Colorado Springs where NASA astronaut Lacy Veach delivered a message of hope about the future to the young people. The Honors Convocation serves at least two valuable purposes. It allows for recognition of significantly more young people, and it brings together at least 100 talented young people with a significant adult who delivers a message of hope for the future. More than 500 students wrote and entered scenarios in the second year of the project. The deliberate emphasis on the positive seemed to work. A large number of students polled at the Honors Convention indicated that they were more positive in attitudes about the future as a result of researching, preparing, and writing a scenario.

(Fig. 6.2 continues on page 114.)

Fig. 6.2—*Continued*

INVENTING THE FUTURE

While the first year stimulated young people to think about the future, and the second year added the crucial element of positivism, the third year accentuated the importance of personal contribution and effort in shaping the future. "Invention: The Heartbeat Of The Future" implied that students could impact the future through their own creative efforts. Basically, students were asked to imagine a time in the future when an invention of *their* own creation would positively impact the world. Their scenarios were to describe how their inventions would make significant contributions. Once again, the number of entrants doubled. Many teachers used the scenario as the culminating student product of multidisciplinary inquiries accenting futures and/or inventions. More than 1,000 youths wrote scenarios about inventions and innovations. The scenarios were not only positive in tone, they were instructive as to the kinds of inventions and innovations young people are imagining. The winning scenario in the K-3 division described a gravity-free playground of the future which served not only as an innovative recreational space for children, but doubled as a tool to train future astronauts. "We will practice exercising, playing, eating, and learning in our own little piece of outer space," wrote Jason, the 8 year-old author. Jason even built a prototype of his zero-gravity playground. One 7 year-old girl described organic shoes. In Amy's future world no one would ever have to worry about having comfortable, serviceable shoes. Children would be fitted at birth with special shoes made of organic material which would keep pace with each person's growth throughout life. A sixth grader's winning scenario proposed the MMCI—MicroChip Conscience Insertion—as one way to develop greater harmony among peoples of the Earth. People would be equipped with a microchip which would cause them to develop exceptional care and compassion for others. Another winning elementary scenario described a "skills machine" which would help people continuously retool and retrain as their current occupations became obsolete in a world where technology is changing rapidly. One of the winning scenarios in the secondary division described a typical day in the life of a future surgeon who invented and utilized a "lazermold" medical technique which could soften the molecular structure of damaged bones, reshape them, and harden them back to a healthy condition. Young people's inventions were not limited to technological breakthroughs. Some youths proposed educational plans to better educate people of all ages in the future, while others suggested new political techniques to end conflicts between governments around the world. The scenarios revealed the genuine desire young people have for playing a role in shaping the world of tomorrow.

An analysis of the scenarios revealed some interesting comparisons between the thinking of boy and girl entrants and between entrants compared across grade levels. Comparison of scenarios written by males and females revealed that boys are nearly twice as apt to write about transportation inventions as girls, while girls are much more likely to imagine inventions categorized as home appliances. Across grade levels, secondary students are nearly three times as likely to write about inventions dealing with science and medicine as are elementary-age students. Conversely, nearly all the inventions categorized as games and toys were found in scenarios written by elementary entrants. Ninety percent of the inventions written about in scenarios could be easily fit into six categorical types: communications, toys and games, home appliances, warfare, transportation, science and medicine.

CONCLUSIONS

The Scenario Writing Project has many benefits, not the least of which is that it promotes healthy, positive images of the future. The project is easily replicable, and it is a fine model of business and education cooperation. Any community with a newspaper can duplicate our effort. If a local newspaper is not anxious to participate in such a project, publication of the winning scenarios in broadsheet or booklet form could become a worthy PTO/PTA project. Idea generating for scenarios can spark exciting classroom discussions which motivate students to engage in research relative to current and projected science and technology. Families become involved, too. Students of winning scenarios indicate they get some of their best ideas from family discussions prompted by the Scenario Project themes. The Scenario Writing Project may not create the nation's future inventors, but it offers more hope than pessimism and negativistic thinking. Students who are encouraged to dream and plan our tomorrows are well on the way to making such dreams come true.

Fig. 6.2. Scenario writing project outlined.

PROJECT LASERMOLD
by Scott Sweet

Seventeen years.

It seems like a million years ago that I entered the medical profession as a reconstructive surgeon. That was back in 1993. Ten years later I joined the staff of the Mayo Clinic in Rochester, Minnesota. The worst medical cases are sent there.

I can't figure out why, but one case stands out. Seven years ago there was a labor demonstration in a Minnesota crystalloy factory. Some fanatic took it too far. He threw a grenade into a scrap heap. It wasn't meant to harm anyone.

So what?

John Drake was walking by the heap when the 4.4-second timer ran out, hurling nearly 1,000 pounds of crystalloy into, and in some spots through, Drake's body.

He was found two hours later by a foreman. He couldn't speak or move. He lay there semi-conscious, in shock.

A Medivac helicopter brought Drake to us. I transferred him to intensive care. Then we knew we had to think of something. He was too far gone to delegate him to a local hospital. It would take so many operations to put Drake's broken body back in form that his life would be endangered as a result.

Three days later I was sitting in my bedroom. Just thinking, trying to grasp the farthest possibility of saving Drake's life. What happened to him was wrong, and I couldn't stop smouldering over it. I went back to the Clinic Sunday morning, determined to do something, anything.

Serendipity is the only way to describe what happened next. I was looking through general information on the crystalloy plant. The two parts of crystalloy (crystal and tungsten) are combined by molecular disruption, not furnace heat. Direct heat damages the reflective qualities. The plant uses a low-power laser to disrupt, but not alter, the structure of the materials. At that point melding the two together is simple.

It hit me like a baseball bat.

Why not do the same to reshape human bone? To use the same disruption process would allow much faster, easier reconstruction.

It took me a while to push the idea through. The clinic staff was a little reluctant to practice any new surgical methods. Malpractice suits were as bad in 2013 as in the latter half of the 20th century, their most rampant time. Eventually my colleagues saw the gravity of John Drake's condition, and committed themselves to the project.

By this time, John could speak. His words clinched the situation.

"Doctor Cahn, do what you wanna do. I've got nothing to lose. I can't move. I can't even turn my head to see you."

His voice broke at that point.

"Do what you can to bring me back."

He was willing to go through with it and so was I.

The staff and I agreed on a date of March 3. Four weeks.

I spent three of those four weeks setting up the operating room. To operate the laser system would require crystalloy technicians to participate in the surgery. I instructed two engineers in the conditions that had to be maintained. They gave me an estimate of how long the bone disruption would take: 10 minutes. Great. The whole operation would only take an hour and a half. This mean less anesthetic would be used and the body would recover faster.

At a press conference before the operation, the Mayo Clinic provided the press with illustrated supplements explaining the "lasermold" surgical process. A summary of the process can be read on the next two pages.

1. Patient is put under and laser disrupter is charged, then placed at point of incision to soften molecular structure of bone.

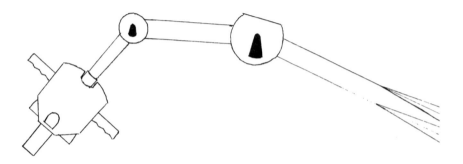

(Fig. 6.3 continues on page 118.)

Fig. 6.3—*Continued*

2. Laser is focused on deformed/damaged bone for 10 minutes. Bone malleability: 8 minutes.

3. Bone(s) harden(s) for twelve hours.

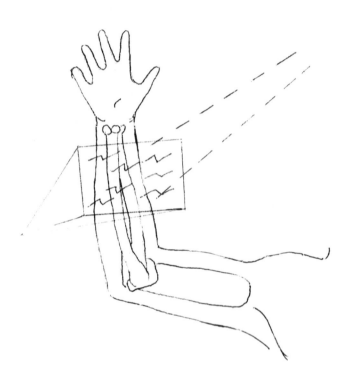

Now the general public knew what was going on. It was up to my team and me to pull it off.

March 2.

The day before "lasermold." All I could do was sweat and worry. I came up against all the doubts and "what ifs" I had ever experienced in med school and in the past seventeen years. My wife set me straight with nine words:

"Have as much faith in yourself as John does."

Yep. I had to. For John Drake.

I woke up five hours later. 6:00 a.m. Time to get ready for the operation.

Drake was brought into the OR at 10:30 a.m. The team I handpicked put him under. I began the surgery with a laser incision. This is called "bloodless surgery" because all veins are cauterized in the area of the incision. I had his torso fixed in forty-two minutes, leaving the bones as well-formed as they were before, needing only to harden for twelve hours. Another forty minutes, and Drake's body was all his once again. Total time: one hour, thirty-four minutes, eleven seconds. When Drake was taken out of the room, the laser was shut down, and we all stared at each other through the sweat running down our forehead and stinging our eyes. This was the revolutionary event in reconstructive surgery.

Six weeks later, with tight rehab, John Drake walked out of the Mayo Clinic. Back into the world.

The press brought up every imaginable benefit of lasermolding. Even some I hadn't thought of. Patients only had to be worked on once, not fourteen or fifteen times. Babies born with genetic defects could be fixed without any problems. Since the surgery was "bloodless," more blood was left available for transfusions and catastrophies. The patient was also in less danger of receiving too much anesthesia, as the operation was much shorter. Another plus was the fact that shackle pins and magnesium joints were not needed as often. Occasionally the body rejects foreign implants.

I retire to a career as Professor of Medicine at UCCS with one dominating thought: Bone deformities are only temporary now.

Fig. 6.3. "Project Lasermold"—scenario. Text and illustrations by student Scott B. Sweet. Used with permission.

IT Arrived in 2031
by Scott Veirs

Arthur Rubey had gotten a window seat, but there wasn't going to be much of a view. After entering the number four boarding portal, he had walked briskly down the ochre-hued isle to the 131st row where, his eyes glinting with anticipation and pride, he seated himself in the window seat, 1310.

From the moment he had set foot on the capsule-shaped Intercontinental Transport (IT), Rubey had appeared totally familiar with the ship's odd doors and strange pure-white corridors and accessories. He did not falter in the least when the shiny portal android asked for and analyzed his boarding disk nor when he strode through the neoteric grid of neon-red beams of the WeaponCheck. Behavior of this sort would have been considered very peculiar indeed for anyone but Arthur. After all, he had designed the entire IT system. IT was his brain child.

Arthur Rubey's Intercontinental Transport was a real innovation in Earth's transportation networks. IT was an idea that no one had pursued or even suggested before. IT was an invention. IT was a particularly rare invention in that while it could take a thousand commuters from New York to London in forty-two minutes, it was almost perfectly efficient! IT was the ultimate in world-wide travel. IT was the ultimate in shipping services, food distribution, tourist transport, and commuter transit. IT had thousands of possibilities. The Arabs would jump at the chance to send super tanker versions of the Transport carrying hundreds of thousands of barrels anywhere in the world in forty-two minutes. IT could be used to transfer food, water, and materials to countries in distress. An incredibly fast world-wide parcel service could be imagined. Anything that was ever moved before could be moved faster now.

The first Intercontinental Transport was designed and built as a capsule that was twenty feet in diameter and two-hundred feet long. IT carried a maximum of 1000 travelers or 6000 cubic feet of payload from New York to London or vice versa at speeds of up to 5,750 miles per hour. IT was a subway of tremendous proportions. At its deepest point, the two-hundred foot long N.Y.-London capsule would be 147 miles under the surface of the Atlantic Ocean, deep within the Earth's mantle. Everyone agreed that, if IT were to work, IT would be the greatest thing since the first Orbitar Space Colony back in 2013.

The IT system was based on the idea that if an object were dropped into a frictionless hole that went straight through the Earth, the object would accelerate until it reached the center and then decelerate until it emerged on the opposite side, where it would be standing still again. Because of the difficulties involved with digging tunnels through molten metal, the tunnels had to be dug along linear paths through the Earth's mantle which was hot, but solid. In these tunnels the object would not "drop" through to the other side. To counteract the force which would pull the object into the bottom of its tunnel an electromagnetic track was placed underneath the object to repel it off the bottom. Horizontal and vertical stabilizers were placed around the object to keep it from bouncing off the walls. All these tracks were powered by forty geo-thermal powered electric generators which were fed by the mantle's high temperatures. Thus the capsule, after the air had been pumped out of the tunnel to eliminate air friction, would slide "downhill" on its track accelerating to the middle of the tunnel and then "uphill," decelerating, until it again came to rest on the surface at its destination.

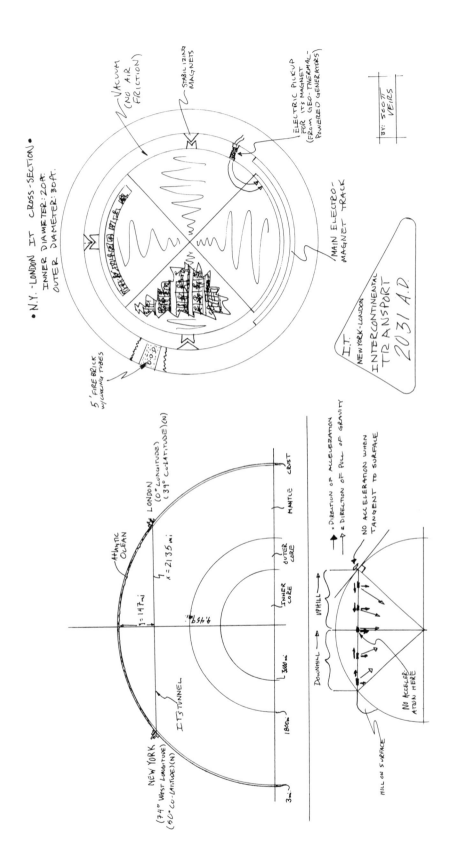

(Fig. 6.4 continues on page 122.)

Fig. 6.4—*Continued*

Before IT's construction was actually begun, there was a lot of "ground" work that had to be done. When the Rubey's backers' researchers returned from the mid-Atlantic with results which confirmed Rubey's temperature and density estimates, the Intercontinental Transport system was given the go-ahead and granted five-hundred million IRCs (Internationally Recognized Currency) over a three year period. The first step was to establish a stable tunnel approximately 2,150 miles long and thirty feet in diameter between New York and London. The newest in mining mechanisms, two nuclear-powered monsters called "John Henrys" with ten meter wide diamond-tipped tungsten carbide bits and multiple high-energy plasma beams and a fleet of highspeed "DumpShuttles," were purchased and put to work in early 2028. One of the monsters was sent straight down 3,000 feet from a cleared block in greater downtown New York City and set on a rectilinear course towards a point half way across the North Atlantic. The other was sent down 3,000 feet below central Hyde Park and coordinated to rendezvous with the first in two years. The high-tech John Henrys each removed four billion cubic feet of crushed rock in those two busy and anxious years at a rate of almost five and a half million cubic feet per day. Each John Henry was followed by a huge "tiler" which laid a five foot thick wall of reinforced firebrick consisting of thirty-five million keystone-shaped bricks interlaced with a hundred thousand miles of cooling tubes. The result was a perfectly straight 2,000 mile long tunnel which was maintained at a comfortable eighty-five degrees Fahrenheit.

During the two years that the tunnels were being drilled, the electromagnetic track, air locks, and AlphaIT, the N.Y.-London capsule, had been assembled. In early 2030, right on schedule, a crew of roller-mounted smart-droids began laying the track and constructing the geo-thermal powered electric generators in each of the fifty foot alcoves spaced at five-hundred mile intervals along the tunnel. At the same time, the first two IT stations were built and the airlocks sealed on the ends of the tunnel. Mid-way through the year, as the smart-droids neared conjunction in the Mid-Atlantic, the final remnants of air were pumped out of the tunnel and the pumps left running on low.

Thus, on the sixth of March, 2031 A.D., just after AlphaIT had been prepared for its first run, Arthur Rubey sat down in his swiveling window seat 131D, smiled, and felt that he had done the world a good turn.

Fig. 6.4. "IT Arrived in 2031"—scenario. Text and illustration by student Scott R. Veirs. Used with permission.

IMAGINEERING

Walt Disney was but one of many people who have used the word "imagineering" to convey the notion or thought of creative individuals engineering and inventing the future. Creative and gifted students can surely experiment with imagineering.

Imagine H. G. Wells's time machine is fact rather than fiction. Transport students into the future and ask them to imagineer tomorrow's homes. It may be well to begin with the familiar. The teacher can ask students to list all the primary functions performed in today's homes. Such functions include preparing and eating food, bathing and personal hygiene, sleeping, waste disposal, sheltering, and clothes maintenance. Next, ask students to list all the inventions which have been invented to facilitate each of these functions. Refrigerators, bath tubs, clothes dryers, and water beds are just a few such inventions. The imagineering begins as students begin to think about and then draw and design new inventions to accomplish these and similar home functions in the future. Provide target dates which are not so far in the future they prohibit any realistic imagineering or so near in time that the inventions created are little more than simple variations of things found in today's homes. Some of the following questions may further aid students in their imagineering exercise.

What will future homes look like, inside and out?

What types of construction materials will be used in home building?

Will future homes have yards and other exterior features common in the 20th century?

What will a typical residential street look like?

Describe each room of the typical home of the future. What new inventions will be found in the kitchen, the bathrooms, the laundry room, the bedrooms, and in the common leisure living area?

Describe a home entertainment center which may be located in the home of the future.

How will the home be heated or cooled?

Design a display advertisement for furniture and appliances which might appear in a newspaper of the future, and that the owners of the typical future home might consult.

While the use of imagery as a classroom technique has been criticized by some religious groups, the author has found it to be a highly effective tool to use for imagineering. The exercise begins with the playing of soothing background music like Pachelbel's "Canon." Students are instructed to be silent, to close their eyes, and to relax. Slowly, the teacher narrates a trip through time to visit a city of the future. Students are asked to imagine and think about the transportation devices utilized on their trip. They are asked to note things like city parks, the kinds of work in which people are engaged, and the architecture in the city. The journey takes them to a school. What things do they see there? They visit a home of a citizen of the city (see figure 6.5). What new inventions do they note in the home? Finally, they get back on the transportation device they have used to travel forward in time and return back to the classroom. Before any sharing is done in the group, each

Fig. 6.5. A future home designed through imagineering.

student is asked to individually note all the things imagined as well as to draw at least one picture of what was seen. This immediate cataloging of the images prevents each student's set of images from being "contaminated" by the oral comments of others. Typically, students are quite surprised at how vivid their images can be.

FUTURE ARCHAEOLOGISTS

Today's archaeologists study the tools and inventions of peoples who lived long ago. Ask students to imagine what future archaeologists may think and write about today's tools, gadgets, and inventions. For example, what will archaeologists in the year 3200 think of the plastic sporks (combination spoon and fork) routinely provided at some fast food restaurants? A particularly hilarious example of just such a probe is found in David Macaulay's *Motel of the Mysteries*, a book which gifted middle and high school students adore. Macaulay, famed for his books about structures such as castles, bridges, and pyramids, has a future archaeologist examine a contemporary motel room and all it contains. The toilet seat is presumed to be a sacred collar worn in a religious ceremony and the ubiquitous plastic fern is classified as "the plant that would not die."[4] Students can take any contemporary institution (e.g., a fast food restaurant, a college football stadium, a television or radio station, a high school building, a mall, etc.) and examine it with a fresh, future-focused pair of eyes. How might scientists of the far future analyze today's inventions? The final product might be a quasiscientific paper, a "learned" lecture before an archaeological society meeting, or a newsworthy cover story for a news magazine like *Newsweek* or *Time*.

FUTURES WHEELS

Much like the webbing process utilized in the introduction of this book, the futures wheels is a tool used by futurists to examine things holistically in order to see the "big picture." An event or issue is placed in the hub or center of the futures wheel. The spokes which radiate outward from the hub are the many consequences which may occur as a result of the primary event. Both positive and negative consequences are considered, with particular attention paid to the possible, ultimate ramifications of each posited consequence. The latter forces participants to consider long-term as well as short-term consequences. President Kennedy and his chief advisors are purported to have used the futures wheel technique in determining the course of action to take when U.S. reconnaissance planes detected Soviet missiles in Cuba in 1962.

The world is shrinking rapidly and long past is the day when the inventor or scientist could remain sequestered in the laboratory blithely unconcerned about the impact his or her invention would have upon the world. Fields which once seemed quite unrelated are now bound together. Inventions in medical technology now force questions in medical ethics. Scientists and philosophers have to sit down with each other and grapple with such issues. Futures wheels allow people to examine the impact of new technologies on many diverse aspects of life, many disciplines, and to consider both short- and long-term effects.

Figure 6.6 is an example of a futures wheel. The central event asks how the invention of increasingly intelligent robots will impact life as we know it today. Multiple considerations are noted.[5]

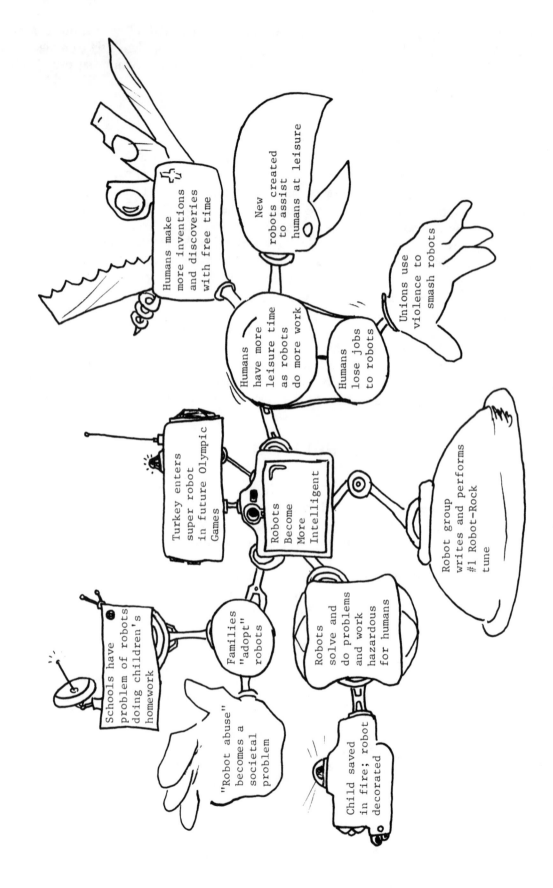

Fig. 6.6. A futures wheel.

Many activities can grow out of the futures wheel activity. Virtually all of the consequences suggested are hypothetical. Students can use the futures wheel activity as the catalyst for research efforts to determine the likelihood of the various hypotheses becoming reality. Thinking about consequences may be just the grist some students need to begin thinking about the plot or theme for an imaginative science fiction story. The artists in the class may be inspired to illustrate some of the hypotheses. The various hypotheses advanced can be examined through the use of the Delphi poll. For example, given certain possible future scenarios about the impact of intelligent robots, what do both lay and expert groups believe will happen. Certainly, a futures wheel exercise may suggest yet still newer inventions. If a particular consequence appears likely and does not appear to be a welcome change, can students invent alternatives?

A final thought. The World Future Society catalog should be in the classroom collection of materials about inventions, especially if the future is to be accented. The catalog lists films, books, and other materials available relative to the study of the future across many disciplines. For a copy of the catalog, write: World Future Society, 4916 St. Elmo Avenue, Bethesda, Maryland 20814.

NOTES

[1]U.S. Department of Commerce Patent and Trademark Office "Project XL" brochure. Specifically, Project XL states that its long-term objective is: "to insure our nation's position as a world leader as we enter the 21st Century—to guarantee that Americans will have the innovative skills to meet the challenges of an increasingly competitive world." For a copy of the brochure, write Project XL: A Quest for Excellence, Washington, D.C. 20231.

[2]B. Edward Shlesinger, Jr., *How to Invent: A Text for Teachers and Students* (New York: IFI/Plenum Data Corporation, 1987).

[3]Joseph J. Corn and Brian Horrigan, *Yesterday's Tomorrows: Past Visions of the American Future* (New York: Summit Books, 1984). *See also*: Paul Lancaster, "Crazy About Invention," *American Heritage of Invention & Technology* 1, no. 1 (Summer 1985): 42-53. Lancaster recounts the contributions of *Popular Mechanics* to the world of inventing from 1902 onward.

[4]David Macaulay, *Motel of the Mysteries* (Boston: Houghton Mifflin, 1979).

[5]For a somewhat different version of the futures wheel, see: Jerry D. Flack, *Hey! It's My Future* (O'Fallon, Mo.: Book Lures, 1986), 10-12.

7

Invention Contests and Programs

In the past decade, several independent trends and events have occurred which appear to have had considerable bearing on the subjects of gifted students and invention and inventing.

Programs for the gifted have rapidly increased in number across the United States and Canada in recent years, and the majority of these programs have been of the enrichment, pull-out type.[1] Since gifted children and adolescents are most often pulled from the mainstream for the delivery of services, it is incumbent that the curriculum provided for them should be qualitatively different from the content and activities offered in regular classrooms. Dr. Joseph S. Renzulli of the University of Connecticut has been one of many gifted child education leaders who has voiced a concern that gifted learners should be producers rather than just consumers of information. His popular Triad Model, widely used in programs for the gifted and talented, emphasizes independent inquiries and product developments wherein gifted students behave as working professionals.[2] As teachers of the gifted have searched for significant and relevant topics and product-oriented outlets, invention has become a natural focus. The subjects of invention and inventing have not been typically found in mainstream education. Further, programs such as Odyssey of the Mind, Invention Conventions, and Invent America provide gifted students with excellent opportunities to display their considerable ingenuity in forums which have simultaneously generated considerable positive publicity for gifted programs.

In a wider arena still, concern for the future of American ingenuity and enterprise has also been a major focus in the past decade. *A Nation at Risk* begins:

> Our nation is at risk. Our once unchallenged preeminence in commerce, industry, science, and technological innovation is being overtaken by competitors throughout the world.[3]

This concern is not unfounded. According to the *Statistical Abstracts of the United States 1988*, foreign companies and individuals received 45 percent of all patents issued by the U.S. Patent Office in 1986.[4] Individuals and groups, representing both government and private sectors, have called for greater emphasis to be placed upon science, math, and technological literacy in American education. One such call for action and reform came from the Carnegie Foundation for the Advancement of Teaching. Ernest L. Boyer reported the Carnegie Foundation's finding that American secondary education needs "to take full advantage of the information revolution and link technology more effectively to teaching and learning in the schools."[5]

Some groups have not been reluctant in identifying causes for the nation's purported decline in ingenuity. A report by the U.S. Commerce Department Technical Advisory Board specifically held America's educational institutions accountable for its treatment of the gifted and talented students, and the role such treatment has played in the decline of innovation in the nation.

> In their march toward egalitarianism, public schools have neglected the special needs of the academically gifted and unusually talented from whom innovations are most likely to come.[6]

The convergence of these trends—the growth of programs for the gifted and talented and the growing criticism of American education—appears to figure prominently in the emergence and rapid growth of international, national, state, and local programs and contests which promote inventing as a valued activity for students. Many such programs specifically target and serve gifted students. Several of these programs will be discussed briefly in this chapter. In addition, guidelines for evaluating invention programs and contests are suggested. A recommendation for the creation of a noncompetitive invention-oriented school program is also discussed.

DIFFUSION NETWORKS

Two national diffusion networks have been created to serve as clearinghouses for information about invention programs. Project XL is an outreach program of the U.S. Patent and Trademark Office. The theme of Project XL is "A Quest for Excellence," and its thrust is the combination and confluence of efforts by education, business, and government to create in today's youth a greater awareness of the importance of technology to the progress of America as the nation prepares to enter the 21st century. Project XL counts among its long-range goals the national coordination of efforts to teach inventive thinking, the dissemination of an informational guide called the Inventive Thinking Project, and the creation of curriculum materials designed to promote critical and creative thinking processes and problem-solving skills. For further information about Project XL, teachers and school library media specialists should contact: Project XL, The Commissioner of Patents and Trademarks, Department of Commerce, Washington, D.C. 20231. The telephone number is (703) 557-3071. At present, the director of the program is Don Kelly.

In cooperation with Project XL, the Study of Innovative Programs for Inventors at the Argonne National Laboratory has produced a "Catalog of Junior Inventor Programs" which describes a wide array of programs which assist junior inventors. The catalog is a product of an ongoing project at Argonne National Laboratory sponsored by the Energy Related Inventions Program (ERIP) of the U.S. Department of Energy. The catalog serves as a clearinghouse for model national, state, and local projects which facilitate invention training for young people. The first edition contains descriptions of 18 different programs. A uniform format provides readers and prospective implementers with single-page descriptors of invention programs, program features and attributes, and contacts for further information. For information about the catalog and the services of this network, contact: Marty Bernard, Energy and Environmental Systems Divisions, Mail Stop 362-2B, Argonne National Laboratory, Argonne, Illinois 60439.

NATIONAL COMPETITIONS

Invent America! is a national educational program and competition for students in grades K-8, which is sponsored by the U.S. Patent Model Foundation. The national headquarters are in Washington, D.C., and the program is directed by Nancy J. Metz. The Invent America! program has among its goals the teaching of problem-solving skills through the invention process. It provides classroom teachers with instructional materials and sponsors an annual conference for teachers devoted to creativity training. Students enter the competition at the building level by providing written descriptions and photographs of models of their inventions. Individual schools send one winning entry per grade level on to state and regional level competitions. Ultimately, national winners are recognized and their models are displayed at the Smithsonian Institution. For complete information about Invent America!, contact: Nancy Metz, Executive Director, Invent America!, 1331 Pennsylvania Avenue, Northwest, Suite 903, Washington, D.C. 20004. The telephone number is (202) 737-1836.

The Invention Convention is a national program for students in grades 1-6 which is sponsored by Silver Burdett and Ginn. The program emphasizes a five-step procedure which includes learning about inventors, finding an idea, research, development and testing, and the culminating Invention Convention. The conventions may be held within classrooms, within schools, and within districts. Forms, procedures, and guidelines are available from Silver Burdett and Ginn. For further details about the Invention Convention program, contact: International Invention Convention, Attention: Science Product Manager, 250 James Street, Morristown, New Jersey 07960. The telephone number is (201) 285-7894.

The Weekly Reader National Invention Contest is a national contest open to students in grades K-12. Again, the competition begins in the classroom. Students submit drawings and photos of their inventions. Classes pick one representative winning entry which is forwarded to the national competition. Originality, usefulness, workability, and clarity of presentation are the standards by which entries are judged. Two grand prize winners are chosen at the elementary and middle school/secondary levels. Winning entries are displayed in Washington, D.C. at the National Inventors Expo. For complete information, contact: Dr. Irwin Siegelman, Editorial Director, Weekly Reader National Invention Contest, 245 Long Hill Road, Middletown, Connecticut 06457. The telephone number is (203) 638-2400.

Although it is not exclusively devoted to inventing, in the traditional sense of the word the Odyssey of the Mind (OM) program involves students in many invention-oriented problem solving tasks. The program began in 1978 at Glasboro State College in New Jersey. It has rapidly mushroomed into one of the most visible projects extant which emphasizes creativity and problem solving in education. In particular, OM has become a staple in programs for gifted students in the United States and Canada. OM has been featured in the CBS series, "I, Leonardo," and in the PBS series, "Creativity with Bill Moyers." IBM recently became the corporate sponsor of this innovative program. Students compete in teams, typically made up of five students, in three grade-level: K-5, 6-8, 9-12. A college division also exists. Four to five long-term problems per division are created each year for students to solve. A typical problem presented to students is to design and build a balsa wood bridge or structure which will support several hundred pounds of weights. Throughout much of the school year students experiment with different approaches to a given problem, attempting to arrive at a best solution. In the spring, competitions begin in schools, cities, and states. These competitions lead to a world finals competition held annually on a major university campus. Several thousand students, parents, and teachers attend the world finals. As with many of the other competitions, curriculum materials for classroom lessons related to the specific problems have been developed and are available to teachers whose teams participate in the program. For further information, contact: Odyssey of the Mind, OM Association, Inc., P.O. Box 27, Glassboro, New Jersey 08028.

STATE COMPETITIONS

In addition to the national programs, several states feature statewide contests and programs. The Minnesota Inventors Congress supports local invention fairs and sponsors the statewide invention fair for students in grades 4-12, which coincides with the Inventors Congress which is for adults. For details, contact Penny Becker, Coordinator, Minnesota Inventors Congress, P.O. Box 71, Redwood Falls, Minnesota 56283-0071. The New York State Department of Education sponsors Imagination Celebration/Invention Convention for all New York state students in grades 6-9. Students describe their inventions in the form of patent applications, which are reviewed by judges at the school building level. An inventor is chosen from each school to present his or her invention at the state-level creativity festival. For further information, contact: Dr. Vivianne Anderson, Imagination Celebration Patent Office, Room 9B38, Cultural Education Center, Empire State Plaza, Albany, New York 12230. The telephone number is (518) 473-0823. One of the oldest and best-known state competitions is the Mini-Invention Team Contest for students in grades K-9 in New Jersey. The project is part of the innovative Technology for Children Program which is housed in the State Department of Education's Vocational Education Division. Students must keep detailed notes about their inventions in a log book, tell why their invention is useful and needed, and must build a model of their invention. Student inventions are judged at local, regional, and state levels. For further details contact: Sylvia Kaplan, Director, Mini-Invention Team (MIIT) Contest, Technology for Children, Division of Vocational Education, New Jersey Department of Education, 225 West State Street, Trenton, New Jersey 08625. Telephone is (201) 290-1900.

SHOULD YOU PARTICIPATE

While the many competitions no doubt serve as catalysts to promote inventing among today's youth, there is understandable concern among growing numbers of educators and parents about the appropriateness of such competitions. Wise teachers will carefully examine the rules and operating procedures of such competitions and observe these programs as they are translated into action at local levels to determine which, if any, of the programs will best serve the needs of their gifted students. Happily, there are many existing programs and hence an exciting menu of options from which to choose. The following critical points may serve as criteria to guide such observations.

Programs should have clear and explicit instructions about how the program is to be implemented as it is terribly unfair to students not to have clear rules to follow. The rules should in precise language prohibit unwarranted expenditures of money, and/or excessive intrusions of adult input and technical assistance. The invention should be that of a student, not his or her parent. The selection of judges is also a critical issue. They must have considerable knowledge and expertise with science and technology. Too often "warm bodies" are substituted for qualified judges who possess the know-how and critical eye needed to spot true ingenuity and originality. Perhaps the most critical issue is the degree of emphasis placed on the competition phase of the project. Sadly, some interscholastic competitive programs seem to miss the fundamental point that it is the learning of skills and processes not the winning of blue ribbons that ultimately counts. If the competition phase becomes the only focus of a program, significant learning outcomes for students are probably lost. When a school or program expends the all of its energies to raise thousands of dollars to send one or two students across the country for a national competition, the degree of real learning is highly suspect. Finally, when state and national programs are the focus, it is vital to observe how the program is run at the local level. A program may have an excellent track record at the state or national level but may not be operated well locally. No matter how fine the national program, students are not well served if the local version is haphazardly organized and administered.

Students do not have to be competing with one another within the classroom, or even outside their school, to enjoy the benefits of invention fairs and programs. Recently, the author helped three junior high school social studies teachers develop an invention fair for their school. All eighth-grade students were involved in a six-week study of inventing, inventions, and inventors. As a culminating activity, students worked individually or in small groups to develop products in one of four categories. The history category asked students with an interest in that discipline to develop time lines, research papers, or other products which focused upon the development of a single invention. Those students with an interest in sociology developed a product which portrayed the impact an invention has had on society. The class comics could create cartoons in the manner of Rube Goldberg, or make humorous visual statements about the impact of various inventions. Finally, students could build working models of their own inventions.

The school library media center served as the display arena for the student products. The exhibit was visited by the entire student body as well as the parent teacher organization during the three weeks of its display. Formal critiques and feedback were given to students by their respective social studies teacher, but prizes or ratings were not awarded. The project and the culminating display emphasized each student's individual creativity, intellectual growth, problem solving, and personal satisfaction with his or her effort.

Many of the invention tasks suggested in chapter 4 will be especially useful to teachers and school library media specialists who desire to create an invention program which will be specific to one classroom or one school.

Regardless of whether invention programs are competitive, or whether they are held at the classroom, building, district, state, or national level, they are of considerable value in motivating young people to explore the worlds of inventing, inventions, and inventors. They also provide meaningful outlets through which gifted students may display their own innovative talent and compare their problem solving skills and solutions with their peers.

NOTES

[1]June Cox, Neil Daniel, and Bruce O. Boston, *Educating Able Learners: Programs and Promising Practices* (Austin, Tex.: University of Texas Press, 1985).

[2]Joseph S. Renzulli, *The Enrichment Triad Model: A Guide for Developing Defensible Programs for the Gifted and Talented* (Mansfield, Conn.: Creative Learning Press, 1977).

[3]National Commission on Excellence in Education, *A Nation at Risk: The Imperative for Educational Reform* (Washington, D.C.: Superintendent of Documents, 1983), 5.

[4]U.S. Department of Commerce, Bureau of the Census, *Statistical Abstracts of the United States 1988* (Washington, D.C.: Superintendent of Documents, 1987), 518.

[5]Ernest L. Boyer, *High School: A Report on Secondary Education in America* (New York: Harper & Row, 1983), 7.

[6]U.S. Department of Commerce, Commerce Technical Advisory Board, *Learning Environments for Innovation* (Washington, D.C.: Superintendent of Documents, 1980), 8.

Appendix

A RESOURCE BIBLIOGRAPHY

> ... The writings on invention ... are of extraordinarily mixed quality. There seems to be no subject in which traditional and uncritical stories, casual rumours, sweeping generalizations, myths and conflicting records more widely abound, in which every man seems to be interested and in which ... skepticism is at a discount.
> — John Jewkes, David Sawers, and Richard Stillerman,
> *The Sources of Invention*

Adams, James L. *Conceptual Blockbusting: A Guide to Better Ideas.* New York: W. W. Norton & Company, 1979.

An engineer tells how to limber up the mental muscles in order to be inventive.

Asimov, Isaac. *Asimov's Biographical Encyclopedia of Science & Technology.* Garden City, N.Y.: Doubleday & Company, Inc., 1982.

The achievements of 1,500 inventors and scientists are chronicled.

_____. *Future Days: A Nineteenth-Century Vision of the Year 2000.* New York: Henry Holt and Company, 1986.

In 1899, a French artist, Jean Marc Côté, was commissioned to create a series of advertising cards which were visions of the year 2000. Asimov provides commentary and 50 examples of Côté's visions of anticipated technologies.

Ayensu, Edward, ed. *The Timetable of Technology.* New York: Hearst Books, 1982.

Significant discoveries, inventions, and developments in medicine, transportation, and other fields from 1900 to 1980, with predictions through 2000.

Birdsall, Derek, and Carlo M. Cipolla. *The Technology of Man: A Visual History.* London: Wildwood House Ltd., 1979.

Expensive coffee table book which chronicles humankind's technical achievements from the Stone Age to the space age.

Brown, A. E. and H. A. Jeffcott, Jr. *Absolutely Mad Inventions.* New York: Dover Publications, Inc., 1960.

A delightful tour through inventions found in the U.S. Patent Office. Includes eyeglasses for chickens, upper lip shapers, and a device to prevent dogs from worrying sheep.

Brown, Kenneth A. *Inventors at Work: Interviews with 16 Notable American Inventors.* Redmond, Wash.: Tempus Books, 1988.

Inventors of pacemakers, lasers, and microprocessors talk about how they invent new technology.

Burke, James. *Connections.* Boston: Little, Brown and Company, 1978.

Must reading for gifted students interested in the critical role invention has played in history. Based upon the PBS series of the same name.

Caney, Steven. *Steven Caney's Invention Book.* New York: Workman Publishing Company, Inc., 1985.

Caney's highly entertaining and informative book provides information on all aspects of invention. He tells young people how to invent, and also provides a social history of the United States through invention stories.

Clark, Ronald W. *Works of Man: A History of Invention and Engineering, from the Pyramids to the Space Shuttle.* New York: Viking Press, 1985.

Clark chronicles human achievements from prehistoric time to the present.

Corn, Joseph J., and Brian Horrigan. *Yesterday's Tomorrows: Past Visions of the American Future.* New York: Summit Books, 1984.

A compilation of visions of inventions of the future from the 1930s.

de Bono, Edward. *Eureka! An Illustrated History of Invention from the Wheel to the Computer.* New York: Holt, Rinehart and Winston, 1974.

From the abacus to xerography, de Bono chronicles history's inventions.

Feldhusen, John F., and Don J. Treffinger. *Teaching Creative Thinking and Problem Solving in Gifted Education.* 3rd ed. Dubuque, Iowa: Kendall/Hunt Publishing Co., 1985.

Tips, tools, and resources for developing inventive behaviors are found in this classic text.

Garrett, Alfred B. *The Flash of Genius.* Princeton, N.J.: D. Van Nostrand Company, 1963.

High school-level material on great scientific discoveries, including penicillin, insulin, rayon, Teflon, etc.

Gibbs-Smith, Charles. *The Inventions of Leonardo da Vinci.* New York: Charles Scribner's Sons, 1978.

The aeronautical, military, nautical, architectural, and vehicular inventions of Leonardo da Vinci are displayed for the reader to marvel at.

Giscard d-Estaing, Valerie-Anne. *The World Almanac Book of Inventions*. New York: World Almanac Publications, 1985.

This is a complete one-volume encyclopedia of inventions. Over 2,000 inventions are described and ordered into fourteen categories such as medicine, the arts, transportation, and information systems.

_____. *The Second World Almanac Book of Inventions*. New York: World Almanac Publications, 1986.

A fine continuation of the first volume, this catalog of inventions should be found and used in all classrooms.

Gordon, W. J. J., and Tony Poze. *Strange and Familiar*. Cambridge, Mass.: Porpoise Books, 1972.

The Synectics model is explained via classroom strategies.

Gourley, Theodore J., and Samuel Micklus. *Problems! Problems! Problems!* Glassboro, N.J.: Creative Competitions, Inc., 1982.

Problems of invention from the Odyssey of the Mind Program.

Grissom, Fred, and David Pressman. *The Inventor's Notebook*. Berkeley, Calif.: Nolo Press, 1987.

This workbook provides the forms, documentation, and advice the beginning inventor needs to take the invention business seriously.

Hanks, Kurt, Larry Belliston, and Dave Edwards. *Design Yourself*. Los Altos, Calif.: William Kaufmann, Inc., 1978.

Creativity, problem solving, and art lessons are all wrapped into one creatively produced package.

Hanks, Kurt, and Jay A. Parry. *Wake Up Your Creative Genius*. Los Altos, Calif.: William Kaufmann, Inc., 1983.

Another easily read, entertaining guide to creative thinking and problem solving. Many anecdotal stories about invention.

Hart, Michael A. *The 100: A Ranking of the Most Influential Persons in History*. New York: Galahad Books, 1978.

Fascinating vignettes of people who have greatly impacted world history. Many inventors included in the 100.

Hooper, Meredith. *Everyday Inventions*. New York: Taplinger Publishing Co., 1976.

Short, easily read pieces about the invention of both ordinary and extraordinary things.

Jewkes, John, David Sawers, and Richard Stillerman. *The Sources of Invention*. New York: W. W. Norton & Company, 1969.

Perhaps hard to find and more difficult to read, but contains original case histories on many inventions like the transistor.

Jones, David E. *The Inventions of Daedalus: A Compendium of Possible Schemes*. San Francisco: W. H. Freeman & Company, 1982.

A compilation of 129 wacky tongue-in-cheek inventions originally published in *New Scientist*.

Judson, Horace Freeland. *The Search for Solutions*. New York: Holt, Rinehart and Winston, 1980.

This classic journey through 400 years of scientific discovery is a wonderful primer devoted to how humanity solves problems through invention.

Keller, Charles, ed. *The Best of Rube Goldberg*. Englewood Cliffs, N.J.: Prentice-Hall, Inc., 1979.

No study of inventions is complete without a sampling of the master of absurd inventions.

Kivenson, Gilbert. *The Art and Science of Inventing*. New York: Van Nostrand Reinhold Company Inc., 1982.

Kivenson is a U.S. patent agent who has worked in industrial research for companies like Westinghouse, Xerox, and U.S. Steel, making his credibility as a writer about inventing high. Considerable information and insight about obtaining a patent, the invention process, and the psychology of inventing.

Klein, Aaron E., and Cynthia Klein. *The Better Mousetrap: A Miscellany of Gadgets, Labor-Saving Devices and Inventions that Intrigue*. New York: Beaufort Books, Inc., 1982.

Includes accounts of American inventions and progress.

Kuhn, Thomas. *The Structure of Scientific Revolutions*. 2nd ed. Chicago: University of Chicago Press, 1970.

Kuhn popularized the word "paradigm" in this excellent history of science. This is an especially appropriate book for gifted students to read.

Lasson, Kenneth. *Mousetraps and Muffling Cups: One Hundred Brilliant and Bizarre U.S. Patents*. New York: Arbor House Publishing Company, 1986.

Just what it claims: a sampling of invention patents, from the genius of Edison and Ford to diapers for birds.

Leokum, Arkady. *Tell Me Why #1: Answers to Hundreds of Questions Children Ask*. New York: Grosset & Dunlap, 1986.

Answers to hundreds of practical questions students ask can be found in volumes 1-4 of Leokum's series.

Macaulay, David. *The Way Things Work*. Boston: Houghton Mifflin Company, 1988.

A book to entertain and instruct readers about today's technology.

McCormack, Alan J. *Inventor's Workshop*. Belmont, Calif.: Pitman Learning, Inc., 1981.

Twenty-five challenging, fun, invention projects for elementary and junior high students.

McNeil, Mary Jean. *How Things Began*. London: Usborne Publishing, Ltd., 1979.

From money to weapons to time pieces, the author uses colorful time lines to portray the evolution of inventions to young people.

Murphy, Jim. *Weird & Wacky Inventions*. New York: Crown Publishers, Inc., 1978.

Excellent reference work on American inventions. See more of the same in the following text.

―――. *Guess Again: More Weird & Wacky Inventions*. New York: Bradbury Press, 1986.

National Geographic: *Those Inventive Americans*. Washington, D.C.: National Geographic Society, 1971.

The archive photographs found in this volume make the work especially useful for classes examining the history of invention in the United States.

National Geographic. *How Things Work*. Washington, D.C.: National Geographic Society, 1983.

From vending machines to traffic signals, students learn how everyday inventions they encounter work in this National Geographic text.

Nayak, P. Ranganath, and John M. Ketteringham. *Breakthroughs!* New York: Rawson Associates, 1986.

Fascinating stories of modern inventing and marketing, including stories behind the VCR, Toyotas, microwave ovens, and Nautilus fitness equipment.

Nicholls, Peter, David Langford, and Brian Stableford. *The Science in Science Fiction*. New York: Alfred A. Knopf, 1983.

Nicholls provides an excellent overview of the "inventions" found in science fiction.

Osborn, Alex F. *Applied Imagination*. New York: Charles Scribner's Sons, 1953.

The master of brainstorming describes innovation and creative problem solving.

Panati, Charles. *Extraordinary Origins of Everyday Things*. New York: Harper & Row, 1987.

From fairy tales to doughnuts and potato chips to footwear, Panati tells readers the origins of more than 500 things.

Park, Robert. *The Inventor's Handbook: How to Develop, Protect, and Market Your Invention*. White Hall, Va.: Betterway Publications, Inc., 1986.

The title says it all.

Perkins, D. N. *The Mind's Best Work*. Cambridge, Mass.: Harvard University Press, 1981.

A superb discussion of the creative processes. Perkins retells the famed Archimedes "Eureka!" tale and looks at the life of Marie Curie among other things.

Pizer, Vernon. *Shortchanged by History: America's Neglected Inventors*. New York: G. P. Putnam's Sons, 1979.

This juvenile book contains, among other things, a chapter on inventor Dr. Sara Josephine Baker.

Reid, Struan. *Invention and Discovery*. London: Usborne Publishing Ltd., 1986.

The time lines in this excellent text are worth the purchase price, and the reader will find still more bargains in the excellent text.

Richards, Norman. *Dreamers & Doers: Inventors Who Changed Our World*. New York: Antheneum, 1984.

Easily read biographical accounts of Robert Goddard, Charles Goodyear, Thomas Edison, and George Eastman.

Rivkan, Bernard. *Patenting and Marketing Your Invention*. New York: Van Nostrand Reinhold Company, Inc., 1986.

This book is quite technical, but of considerable value to older students.

Scherr, George H., ed. *The Best of the Journal of Irreproducible Results*. New York: Workman Publishing Company, Inc., 1983.

Yet another wild collection of humorous, inventive immodest proposals. Adult humor in some excerpts.

Scholes, Robert, and Eric S. Rabkin. *Science Fiction: History—Science—Vision*. New York: Oxford University Press, 1977.

Literary "inventions" are discussed as the author explores the science found in the favored literary genre of gifted students.

Shlesinger, B. Edward, Jr. *How to Invent: A Text for Teachers and Students*. Alexandria, Va.: IFI/Plenum Data Corporation, 1985.

This definitive book makes the invention process understandable.

Spivack, Doris. *Decide and Design*. Phoenix, Ariz.: Think Ink Publishers, 1982.

Includes creative starting points for young inventors as well as a handy chronology of significant inventions and an excellent bibliography on inventions and inventors.

Stanish, Bob. *The Unconventional Invention Book*. Carthage, Ill.: Good Apple, Inc., 1981.

This book is a primer on invention activities for the elementary grades.

Stanish, Bob, and Carol Singletary. *Inventioneering*. Carthage, Ill.: Good Apple, Inc., 1987.

Many fine ideas for middle school students are included in this book.

Torrance, E. Paul. *The Search for Satori & Creativity*. Buffalo, New York: Creative Education Foundation, Inc., 1979.

A pioneer in the field of creativity writes informatively, but nontechnically about the creative uses of the mind.

Vare, Ethlie Ann, and Greg Ptacek. *Mothers of Invention: From the Bra to the Bomb: Forgotten Women & Their Unforgettable Ideas*. New York: William Morrow & Co., Inc., 1988.

This highly readable book, devoted to women inventors, is a valuable addition to literature on invention.

Villalpando, Eleanor, and Sam Lowe. *Brainstorms*. Phoenix, Ariz.: Think Ink Publishers, 1982.

von Oech, Roger. *A Whack On the Side of the Head*. New York: Warner Books, 1983.

Fresh, lively, practical tips and strategies for realizing greater creative potential are found in von Oech's highly readable book.

_____. *A Kick in the Seat of the Pants*. New York: Perennial Library, 1986.

The author continues to provide sage advice and bright ideas for how to use the mind creatively.

The Way Things Work: An Illustrated Encyclopedia of Technology. New York: Simon and Schuster, 1967.

The working of everything from flatirons to escalators are explained in this fine text first published in Germany.

Williams, Trevor I. *The History of Invention*. New York: Facts on File Publications, 1987.

In addition to serving as an excellent chronicle of human achievements in the field of inventions, the text includes biography capsules of the great inventors and excellent examples of time lines.

Wulffson, Don L. *The Invention of Ordinary Things*. New York: Lothrop, Lee, & Shepard Books, 1981.

The invention of such diverse products as jigsaw puzzles, playing cards, the toothbrush, mirrors, and the alarm clock are related in easy-to-read accounts.

Index